Nawab Sultan Jahan Begam

Her Highness Nawab Sultan Jahan Begam,
Ex-Ruler of Bhopal.

Nawab Sultan Jahan Begam

Ex-Ruler of Bhopal

An Account of My Life

Akhtar Iqbal

Translated By:

C. H. Payne

Reissued by

NIYOGI
BOOKS

Originally Published by The Times Press, Bombay in 1927

Re-issued by

NIYOGI
BOOKS

D-78, Okhla Industrial Area, Phase-I
New Delhi-110 020, INDIA
Tel: 91-11-26816301, 49327000
Fax: 91-11-26810483, 26813830
email: niyogibooks@gmail.com
website: www.niyogibooks.com

ISBN: 978-93-81523-08-7
Publication: 2012

Printed at: Niyogi Offset Pvt. Ltd., New Delhi, India

AUTHOR'S PREFACE

In the first volume of my memoirs, *Gohur-i-Iqbal*[1] I told the story of the first seven years of my reign. The present volume, which I have called *Akhtar Iqbal*, carries the story down to the end of the twelfth year. The former is itself a sequel to the history of Bhopal written by my revered mother, Nawab Shah Jahan Begam, and named *Taj-ul-Iqbal*. Together these three volumes cover a period of over two hundred years, and they thus form a complete record of the origin and history of the Bhopal State, the vicissitudes through which it has passed, and the gradual development, from reign to reign, of its resources and administrative organization. In the following pages, I have endeavoured to give a faithful picture of the general conditions of life in Bhopal to-day, and the manner and character of its administration. This will enable my readers to estimate the possibilities of further progress, and the extent to which I and my people are justified in looking forward with hope to the future

(1) *Gohur-i-Iqbal* (The Pearl of Prosperity) was translated into English by C. H. Payne, and published in 1912 with the title " An Account of My Life " (*London, John Murray*). *Taj-ul-Iqbal* (The Crown of Prosperity) was translated by H. C. Barstow, and published in Calcutta in 1876 (*Thacker, Spink and Co.*). *Akhtar Iqbal*, the Persian title of the present volume, signifies 'The Star of Prosperity.'

TRANSLATOR'S NOTE

LIKE the previous volumes of Her Highness's memoirs, *Akhtar Iqbal*, which is translated in the following pages, is written in Urdu, the language of Her Highness's family, and of the majority of her subjects. Its style is pure and unaffected, and the language is throughout clear, réfined, and vigorous. In addition to a beautifully lithographed copy of the original, Her Highness has been good enough to place at my disposal a literal translation of the major portion of the work, made under her supervision by Mr. B. Ghoshal, an accomplished Urdu and Persian scholar. This has enabled me to check my own translation, and has greatly assisted me in the elucidation of difficult passages.

C. H. P.

CONTENTS

CHAPTER I

The Seventh Year of My Reign

The anniversary of my accession—Dancing parties—The State postal system—The Alexandra High School—The higher education of Chiefs—Honour conferred on Colonel Obaidullah Khan .. .. pp. 1–8

CHAPTER II

Administrative Reforms in 1908

A tour of inspection—The Secretariat—Secretarial staff—Arts and crafts—The Excise Department—Revenue arrears—Position of the *jagirdars*—State treasury looted—Inspection of Imperial Service Troops—Establishment of Advisory Council—Visit of the Prince of Arcot to Bhopal .. pp. 9–17

CHAPTER III

A Year of Progress

Introduction of new land-settlement—Distribution of leases—Rights of *mustajirs*—Need for trained nurses in India—The Lady Minto Nursing School—Indian midwives—Classes opened for instruction in midwifery—Backward state of Indian women—The Princess of Wales Club—The King Edward Museum .. .. pp. 18–30

CHAPTER IV

VISIT OF LORD MINTO TO BHOPAL

His Excellency Lord Minto—Preparing for his visit to Bhopal—Police arrangements—State reception at railway station—Procession to the Lal Kothi—State visits—A military gymkhana .. .. pp. 31–42

CHAPTER V

SOME CEREMONIES AND A BANQUET

A visit to the Sultania Girls' School—Lady Minto's speech—Lady Minto opens the Ladies' Club—Opening of the Alexandra School—Lord Minto's speech—Opening of the King Edward Museum—State banquet at the Rahat Manzil—I propose Lord Minto's health—His Excellency's reply—A military review—A garden-party—The Minto Hall .. pp. 43–58

CHAPTER VI

SPORTS AND A MARRIAGE

I. S. T. Athletic Meeting at Bhopal—A dinner at the Lal Kochi—A marriage procession—Reception of the bride and bridegroom at the Rahal Manzil—Another banquet—After-dinner speeches—Birth of Nur Jahan Begam—Establishment of Land Records Office—Loans to cultivators—Various administrative reforms—I go to Pachmarhi .. pp. 59–75

CHAPTER VII

DEATH OF KING EDWARD VII

Announcement of the King's death—My message of condolence—Mourning in Bhopal—Edward the Peace-maker—His affection for the people of India—The honours he conferred on me—Sorrow in India—Sympathy for Queen Alexandra—Accession of King George V—India's confidence in the new King .. .. pp. 76–82

CHAPTER VIII

ILLNESS OF MY SECOND SON

Col. Obaidullah Khan visits the Viceroy at Calcutta—Is taken ill and returns to Bhopal—Goes for a sea voyage—I take him to Mussoorie for treatment—Funeral of the late King—I attend memorial service—Return with my son to Bhopal—A reassuring report on my son's health.. pp. 83–91

CHAPTER IX

A FAREWELL BANQUET

My views on Chiefs' Colleges—Why I sent my youngest son to Aligarh—My visit to the M. A. O. College—Colonel Daly's departure from Central India—His farewell visit to Bhopal—I entertain him at a banquet and propose his health—Colonel Daly's speech .. .. .. pp. 92–101

CHAPTER X

A VISIT TO SIMLA

I go to Simla—A children's ball at Viceregal Lodge—I am invested with the Order of G.C.S.I.—Lady Dane's purdah party—Paying and receiving visits—Simla weather—Col. Obaidullah Khan's health—Consultation with Surgeon-General Lukis—Birjis Jahan sends Lady Minto a butterfly—Departure from Simla and return to Bhopal. pp. 102–108

CHAPTER XI

CLOSING EVENTS OF THE YEAR 1911

Official visit of Mr. O'Dwyer to Bhopal—Banquet and speeches—Meeting of Daly College Council—My plea for a Chiefs' university—Lord Minto's departure from India—King Edward memorial for Central India—I visit the Allahabad Exhibition and attend first meeting of the Maha Mandal Sabha .. .. pp. 109–118

CHAPTER XII

I ENTERTAIN MY FRIENDS

I celebrate my investiture as G.C.S.I.—I entertain the A. G. G. and other friends—Prize distribution at the Sultania School—My address to the pupils—Another banquet—I propose the health of the A. G. G.—His reply—*Nashra* ceremony of Sahibzadi Birjis Jahan Begam.. pp. 119–129

CHAPTER XIII

SOME MORE ADMINISTRATIVE REFORMS

Improvements to the city of Bhopal—Extension of the water supply—Re-settlement of the Piklon *tahsil*—Failure of the *ryatwari* system—Satisfactory results of new settlement—Condition of the *jagirdars*—Benefits of the *Hit Karini Sabha*—Progress of education—A Kindergarten class. 130–135

CHAPTER XIV

MY FIRST VISIT TO EUROPE

I decide to attend His Majesty's coronation in England—The members of my party—Our journey to Paris—Col. Obaidullah Khan goes to Nauheim—Arrival and reception at Dover—Our house at Redhill—I attend His Majesty's levee—My visit to Queen Alexandra—The coronation service in Westminster Abbey—A garden-party at Buckingham Palace—Presentation of medals to Indian Chiefs and Officers —How I spent my time in London .. .. pp. 136–147

CHAPTER XV

ON THE CONTINENT, AND HOME AGAIN

I proceed to Constantinople—My audience with His Majesty the Sultan—His Majesty takes me to see the Sultana —The sacred relics of Istamboul—Gifts bestowed on me by

His Majesty—Journey from Constantinople to Brindisi—Receive news that plague has broken out in Bhopal—A rough passage to Port Said—I visit Lord Kitchener at Cairo—The Khedive's hospitality—Homeward journey and arrival at Bhopal .. .. pp. 148–155

CHAPTER XVI

I ATTEND THE IMPERIAL DURBAR

My invitation to attend the Imperial Durbar and my reply—The Bhopal camp—My reception at Delhi—I preside at a meeting of the All India Educational Conference—Arrival of Their Imperial Majesties at Delhi—Presentation of Indian Chiefs—Procession to the Imperial camp—I am granted a private audience—My address of welcome—His Majesty lays the foundation-stone of the All India King Edward Memorial—His Majesty presents colours to various regiments—The Coronation Durbar .. .. pp. 156–172

CHAPTER XVII

AT DELHI AFTER THE DURBAR

Reception of Maharanis by Her Majesty the Queen—Garden-party in the Fort—His Majesty shows himself at the *darshan jharokha*—Review of troops—Fine performance of the Bhopal Lancers—Serious indisposition of Col. Obaidullah Khan—He is visited by His Majesty's physician—An investiture ceremony—Her Majesty is invested with the Order of the Star of India—I receive the Order of the Crown of India—His Majesty lays the foundation-stone of the new city of Delhi—Their Majesties leave Delhi—Services of Bhopal troops and officers at the Durbar—My Christmas and New Year's greetings to Their Majesties—How the coronation was celebrated at Bhopal—I bid Their Majesties farewell at Bombay .. .. pp. 173–185

CHAPTER XVIII

The Year 1912

I visit the Viceroy and Lady Hardinge at Calcutta—I receive a deputation from the Islamia Orphanage—My scheme for a memorial of Queen Mary's visit to India—I propose to establish a college for the higher education of women—Result of my appeal for funds—Visit of Sir O'Moore Creagh and Lady Creagh to Bhopal—A military Club for Bhopal—I attend the opening of the new Daly College buildings at Indore—His Excellency Lord Hardinge accepts my invitation to Bhopal .. .. pp. 186–194

CHAPTER XIX

Lord Hardinge's Visit to Bhopal

Connection of Lord Hardinge's family with my State—His Excellency's arrival and reception at Bhopal—Opening of the Hamidia Library—Lady Hardinge visits Girls' Schools and Ladies' Club—State Banquet at which I propose Their Excellencies' health—Lord Hardinge's reply—A military review—His Excellency lays the foundation-stone of the new Military School, and Lady Hardinge that of the Infants' Home—Her Excellency's speech—Garden-party at Ahmedabad—My guests depart—Attempt to assassinate Lord Hardinge—I go to Delhi to express my sympathy and congratulate His Excellency on his escape .. .. pp. 195–219

CHAPTER XX

Other Events of the Years 1911 and 1912

Celebration of the Coronation at Bhopal—The census—I establish a cotton mill—Sir Ibrahim Rahmatullah—Judicial and revenue legislature—Some educational measures—Col. Obaidullah Khan's valuable services in the Military Department—Deaths of some distinguished members of my family—Mian Yasin Muhammad Khan—Mian Hamid Muhammad

Khan—Mian Aqil Muhammad Khan—Deaths of three prominent State officials—Maulavi Nasir-ud-din—Bakhshi Muhammad Hasan—Hakim Syad Nur-ul-hasan. pp. 220–229

CHAPTER XXI

THE SAME CONTINUED

Some distinguished visitors to Bhopal—Sir John Hewett—The Maharaja of Kapurthala—The Maharaja of Gwalior—Lord Sydenham—Sir Henry McMahon—I become patroness of Ladies' Clubs at Lahore and Allahabad—I contribute to the funds of the M. A. O. College hostel—Urgent need of hostels for Muhammadan students—I contribute to the Osmanli Red Crescent Fund—Also to the Moslem University fund—I and my sons assist Maulana Shibli to publish his biography of the holy Prophet .. .. pp. 230–237

CHAPTER XXII

AN HONOUR'S LIST

I acknowledge the services rendered to me and the State by my three sons—My ministers—The officers of the Revenue and Judicial Departments—The officers of the Secretariat—Of the Accounts Department—Of the Educational Department—And of the Military Department .. pp. 238–246

CHAPTER XXIII

GENERAL SURVEY OF THE ADMINISTRATION

Results of the nineteen years' settlement—Present state of the Forest and Customs Departments—Expenditure on the Military Department—The grading of State officers—State roads—Village sanitation—The Bhopal Municipality—Schools and hospitals—Religious instruction in Schools—Progress of female education—The State prisons—The State police—Reforms in legal procedure—Present financial position of the State .. .. p. 247

LIST OF ILLUSTRATIONS

H. H. The Begam of Bhopal	*Frontispiece*	
Edward Museum, Bhopal	*Facing page*	30
The Earl of Minto	,, ,,	40
The Countess of Minto	,, ,,	58
H. I. M. King Edward VII	,, ,,	76
H. M. King George V	,, ,,	82
Queen Alexandra	,, ,,	142
H. M. Queen Mary	,, ,,	178
Lord Hardinge of Penshurst	,, ,,	196
Ladies' Club, Bhopal	,, ,,	204
Lady Hardinge	,, ,,	216

IN THE NAME OF GOD,

THE COMPASSIONATE, THE MERCIFUL

CHAPTER I

THE SEVENTH YEAR OF MY REIGN

WITHOUT any thought of sounding my own praises, I can say that, from the day when, by the grace of Almighty God and the favour of the British Government, the reins of administration were placed in my hands, it has been my constant endeavour to promote the happiness of my subjects and the welfare of my State. I know that I shall be held accountable on the day of judgment for even a single moment's neglect of the responsibilities that have been placed upon me.

I thank God for having given me strength to carry out my duties, and I rejoice to know that my labours have been appreciated by my beloved subjects. Nothing can more amply compensate a ruler for the trials and anxieties of his office than the knowledge that he is increasing the happiness and prosperity of those who live under his sway.

In the year 1326 A.H. (1908 A.D.) when I celebrated, according to custom, the seventh anniversary of my accession to the throne, I received tokens of loyalty and affection from all classes of my people. A large number of congratulatory addresses were presented to me, and garden-parties and dinners were given in honour of the occasion. Amongst the addresses, none gave me greater satisfaction than those I received from the Board of Administration and the *jagirdars*; for the former body is representative of the entire population of the State; while the *jagirdars*, by reason of their rank and their position as landed proprietors, are the most influential of my subjects. In every case the addresses contained warm expressions of loyalty and gratitude for the benefits enjoyed under my administration. This was the first occasion on which the people of Bhopal were enabled thus personally to tender their devotion to their ruler; and I was much impressed by the intellectual and moral progress which their addresses betokened.

On the day of my anniversary, all the students in Bhopal assembled in their respective schools and celebrated the occasion with speeches and other loyal demonstrations. They then came to make their salams to me, and to recite the congratulatory odes which they had composed in my honour. Their loyal and affectionate greetings gave me sincere pleasure, and I prayed to God to enrich their minds with knowledge and wisdom. Before dismissing them I distributed the prizes which had been awarded in each school. I always take a special pleasure in presenting such awards; for on the students in our schools we build all our hopes of future progress. My eldest son, Nawab Nasrullah Khan, founded a scholarship at the Alexandra High School to commemorate this interesting ceremony.

Before passing on to other matters I desire to say a few words in reference to the dancing and singing parties which, as is usual on such occasions, were a prominent feature of these celebrations. I am strongly opposed to the holding of such parties, firstly because they are contrary to the established laws of Islam, and secondly because they involve a scandalous waste of money. If the large sums which were squandered on entertainments of this kind had been devoted to the public good, a lasting and worthy memorial of my reign might have been created. But, as many of my subjects had never before taken part in a State celebration of this kind, I considered that it would be inexpedient and ungracious on my part to interfere with their enjoyment. I was, however, very pleased to observe that none of my three sons attended these parties, though they were much pressed to do so. Indeed, it has always been their habit to abstain from things forbidden by their religion, and to shun unwholesome pleasures. I have always had complete confidence in them; but in this instance their principles were put to a very severe test, and the self-control which they displayed gave me great joy. I do not doubt that they will always meet temptation in the same courageous spirit; and no one can tell the comfort I derive from this thought.

The seventh year of my reign was marked by considerable administrative progress. The most important changes were the reforms I introduced into the postal and educational services.

A State postal system was first established in the reign of my mother. The head office was located in the city of Bhopal, and there were branch offices in the various *tahsils* and *thanas*.[1] Letters were carried by runners or "bangy-wallahs."[2] This system worked well enough in its way; but it lacked many of the features essential to an efficient postal service, and the people enjoyed few of the conveniences and facilities provided by the postal department of British India. I tried my best to effect some reforms, and my efforts were not wholly unsuccessful; but it was evident to me that the Bhopal system was on too small a scale to admit of the improvements I most desired to introduce. Accordingly, in the year 1903, with a view to the greater convenience of my subjects, and in the interests of the trade of the State, I pressed for the amalgamation of the Bhopal department with the Imperial Post Office. After lengthy corres-

(1) A *tahsil* is a subdivision of a revenue district. In the Bhopal State each of the three districts, or *nizamats*, consisted of nine *tahsils*. A *thana* in olden times meant a fortified post; to-day it usually signifies a police station.

(2) A 'bangy' (Sansk. *bahangi*) is a shoulder-yoke. It usually consists of a stout strip of bamboo, with a net or basket at either end for parcels, etc.

pondence with the Government of India, terms satisfactory to both sides were arranged, and on the 1st July, 1908, the amalgamation took place. One or two British post offices had, in the meantime, been opened, and it was arranged that others should be established as the need for them arose, the cost in each case being borne by the British postal department. Stamps sufficient to meet the requirements of the service were to be supplied at cost price. These were to be specially prepared, and were to bear the State's mark. If at any time letters or mail-bags were looted, the loss resulting therefrom was to be made good by the State. The British Post Office undertook to make arrangements for camp post offices whenever the Ruler, or any member of the Ruler's family, went into camp, or whenever the Muin-ul-muham, the Nasir-ul-muham, or other high official, was on tour for State purposes. In regard to the punishment of crime, it was agreed that any employé of the Post office guilty of an offence under the Post Office Act should, if a British subject, be tried before a British court of justice ; but that a subject of the State, whether a post-office employe or not, should, if guilty of a like offence, be tried by the courts of Bhopal.

On the day on which the amalgamation took place, I received visits from the Deputy Director-General of Post Offices in India, the Deputy Postmaster-General, and the Superintendent of Post Offices in the Narbada Division, all of whom came to Bhopal for the occasion. The amalgamation has proved a great blessing to the people of Bhopal, while it has relieved the administration of the upkeep of a department which was a perennial drain on the finances of the State.

To turn now to educational matters. The Alexandra School, of which I have already made mention, was first organized on the lines of a Chiefs' college, and a course of study similar to that followed in the Daly College at Indore was adopted. I was, however, not entirely satisfied with this system. Furthermore, I received from the nobles of Bhopal, for the benefit of whose sons the school had been opened, a petition urging the adoption of the curriculum prescribed for High Schools by the Allahabad University, so as to give their sons a better chance of qualifying for State appointments. After much careful consideration, I came to the conclusion that the suggestion contained in the petition was both reasonable and wise. I accordingly gave orders for the introduction of the High School curriculum, and took such other steps as were necessary to secure the recognition of the school by the university authorities.

These matters recalled to my mind the general question of the higher education of Indian Chiefs, and for several months my mind was continually occupied with this difficult problem. It was while my thoughts were thus engaged that I had the opportunity of being present at a meeting of the

Council of the Daly College. By a happy coincidence, the Hon'ble Colonel Daly, whose illustrious father was the founder of this college, was at this time Agent to the Governor-General in Central India. I knew the deep interest which Colonel Daly took in the Daly College, and also that the education of Indian Chiefs was a subject that invariably aroused his sympathetic attention. I, therefore, determined to make the most of so favourable an occasion; and having embodied my views in a pamphlet, which I had printed both in Urdu and in English, I laid it before the Council for consideration. I also sent copies to the press, and to as many of my friends as I knew to be interested in such matters, desiring them to favour me with their views.

As I had hoped, the pamphlet aroused considerable interest in responsible quarters, and my views, and their bearing on the future of the ruling class, were widely discussed. It was also read and discussed at the Council meeting of the Daly College, and was published and commented upon in many of the leading newspapers and journals. Mr. Waddington, Principal of the Mayo College at Ajmer, and Mr. Wilkinson of the Aitchison College, Lahore, examined my proposals in great detail, and I was much helped by the criticisms of these two educational experts. The chief objections urged against my scheme for a Chiefs' university were dearth of students, and the difficulty of providing the necessary funds. I answered these objections in a second pamphlet, which I placed before the same Council on the 6th April, 1909.

One other event belonging to this year remains to be recorded. My second son, Colonel Obaidullah Khan, had on many occasions been warmly commended by British military officers for the unflagging energy and marked ability he had shown in the training of the State army and the Bhopal Imperial Service cavalry. He had also had the honour of being personally complimented by His Excellency Lord Kitchener, Commander-in-Chief of His Majesty's forces in India, who, during a recent visit to Bhopal, witnessed a review of the troops, and spoke in very high terms of their discipline and efficiency. My son's hard work did not go unrewarded; and in addition to the distinctions already conferred on him, he was now made an honorary Captain in the British army.

CHAPTER II

ADMINISTRATIVE REFORMS IN 1908

IN the year 1907, I personally inspected the working of the settlement in the Eastern and Southern districts of the State. This year, in the course of a four weeks' tour, I made a similar inspection in the Western district. Following my usual practice, I listened to all who had complaints to make, and whenever possible adjusted their grievances on the spot.

It had long been a custom in Bhopal that the Ruler, after dealing with and passing orders on State papers, should sign, or verify by affixing the *suad*, [1] not only the original orders, but every copy of the same that was required for issue. This system entailed much delay and unnecessary work. During my previous tour, I effected some salutary changes; and this year, in order still further to simplify and expedite the despatch of public business, I established a regular secretariat, placing each department of the administration under a separate secretary. The procedure

(1) 'Sad' or 'suad' is the 14th letter of the Arabic alphabet. It is frequently used as an abbreviation for *Sahih*= correct' or 'confirmed.'

to be followed was laid down in a set of rules known as the Secretariat Regulations. Under this system a "docket," or office note, is attached to each paper that is put before me, or a secretary can personally submit to me any paper requiring further explanation. In every case, the orders I pass are issued to the officers concerned in the form of a *marasala*, or official letter. The saving in time and labour thus effected has greatly facilitated the work of administration.

The chief officers of the Secretariat are the Financial, the Judicial, the Military, and the Educational Secretaries, and the Private Secretary to the Ruler. The financial department is in the charge of Syad Mansab Ali, a veteran officer who, though unacquainted with the English language, has a wide and intimate knowledge of revenue matters. He was an officer of my *deorhi* in the days when I was heir-apparent, and was much respected by my husband, Nawab Ihtisham-ul-mulk. He is a native of Kanjpura, and his father had been in the service of the late Nawab Sahib. He served me very faithfully before I came to the throne, and because of my high opinion of his work, I have raised him step by step to his present position. The post of Judicial Secretary is held by Muhammad Hasan Khan, a distinguished graduate of the Aligarh College, who, through his marriage with the sister of Mian Iqbal Muhammad Khan, is now a member of my family. The Military Secretary is Abdu-s Samad Mazhar. He hails from Quetta, and is also a graduate of distinction. Before promotion to his present office, he was secretary to Sahibzada Obaidullah Khan, Colonel-in-Chief of the State forces. He is a man of many parts. Liakat Ali, who holds the post of Educational Secretary, belongs to a highly respected Bareilly family. He was formerly tutor to Sahibzada Muhammad Hamidullah Khan, and prior to his present appointment, filled numerous State offices. Sakhawat Husain, my Private Secretary, is an old servant of the State. He was Assistant Private Secretary to my mother, and from the beginning of my reign he has rendered me faithful and valuable service.

After establishing the Secretariat, I turned my attention to the Public Works department, which had long been in an unsatisfactory condition. In addition to various necessary reforms, I appointed a qualified engineer to supervise the carrying out of all important works. I hope, in the course of a few years, to bring this department into a thoroughly efficient state.

With a view to stimulating trade, a large fair was held this year in Shahjahanabad. I exempted all who opened stalls from the payment of octroi dues on the commodities and animals they imported for sale. The fair lasted for five days; but although it attracted many people, it cannot be said to have achieved the purpose for which it was opened. So long as the spirit of enterprise is wanting, such measures can be productive of little permanent good. In Bhopal, industrial development is a plant of very slow growth. Indigenous arts and crafts show few signs of advance, and cultivators have as yet shown no ambition to improve either the crops they raise, or the cattle they breed. At some future time, when all unoccupied lands have been brought under cultivation, it is my intention to go thoroughly into these matters, and take active and practical steps to develop the industrial and agricultural resources of the State.

This year, I gave instructions to the Forest Department that some rubber and camphor trees were to be planted, by way of experiment, in a garden near the city. If the experiment proves successful, it is my intention to plant both these trees on a more extensive scale, and to cultivate them on scientific lines.

Since the commencement of my reign, I have made various important and salutary reforms in the Excise Department. I have done all in my power to discourage the cultivation of the poppy in the State; but as the opium market remains open, and as the Malwa plateau is the principal opium producing district, definite prohibitive measures have not been taken. Nevertheless, to protect my people as far as possible from the baneful effects of this drug, I issued orders to my Excise officers, and this was while there was still a strong demand for opium in the market, to keep all poppy growers under strict surveillance; and later on, as a further check on the production of the drug, I framed and issued regulations similar to those which were in force in British India. These measures were to a large extent successful. The action of the Bhopal darbar was warmly welcomed by the Government of the Central Provinces, and the Chief Commissioner recorded his appreciation in an official gazette.

Thanks to Almighty God, not only the city of Bhopal, but the entire State was immune from the ravages of plague during this year. There were occasional outbreaks of malaria ; but these were not of a serious description. After the rains, I went to Bombay for a change of air, and spent some ten days at Walkeshwar in a bungalow close to the sea. I had the pleasure of meeting His Excellency the Governor, and several of my friends who resided in Bombay visited me. The change greatly benefited my health.

My return to Bhopal was followed by further administrative reforms. The office of the Naib Muin-ul-muham (Assistant Revenue Minister) was done away with, and was replaced by an office for the collection of arrears of revenue, organized on new and efficient lines, and State regulations were issued to enforce the payment of outstanding dues within a given period. Under this system, defalcations reported by any branch of the administration are investigated forthwith. A defaulter, however, is given ample opportunity to explain or defend his conduct; and it is only after a thorough investigation that a warrant authorizing the recovery of the debt is issued. The establishment of this office has greatly facilitated the work of the Revenue Department. The promptness with which many *mustajirs* and tenants now discharge their obligations shows that the disease of non-payment, which not long ago was rampant in every district of the State, is gradually being stamped out.

The financial position of the *jagirdars*, despite various remedial measures, was at this time far from satisfactory. Nearly every *jagir* was heavily encumbered with debts, and much financial confusion prevailed. With a view to the interests both of the *jagirdars* and their creditors, I this year appointed an Official Receiver to take charge of all attached lands; and at the same time I issued stringent orders that no further debts were to be contracted without the consent of the State. Under the old ruling, when a decree was issued against a *jagirdar*, a third of his estate was liable to attachment. The confiscated portion came under the management of the local *tahsildar*, who paid the creditors out of the revenue derived therefrom. This arrangement was in every way unsatisfactory: the lands deteriorated, the tenants suffered, and there was continuous friction between *jagirdars* and *tahsildars*. Under the new system, the revenue from confiscated lands is collected by the Receiver, who is responsible not only for keeping the accounts and paying the creditors, but for the general upkeep of the property, and the welfare of the cultivators.

In the month of March, gold mohurs to the value of Rs. 2,86,811 were stolen from the State treasury. The robbery was committed by a gang of thieves who had been at work for several days. The money was stored in a strong-room overlooking the lake; and as there was no thoroughfare between the treasury and the lake, they were able to carry out their depredations unperceived. The matter was placed in the hands of the police, who succeeded not only in tracing the thieves, but in recovering practically the whole of the money stolen.

I have already referred to the inspection of the State forces by His Excellency Lord Kitchener, and I must now add a few words regarding the marked progress which the Imperial Service Troops displayed this year in musketry and signalling. The work done in these two branches was highly commended by His Majesty's inspecting officers. In reference to the former, the Assistant Adjutant-General for Musketry reported as follows :—

"All most efficient and keen. The Honorary Colonel Sahibzada Haji Hafiz Obaidullah Khan takes a very great deal of trouble and interest. Results very satisfactory."

The report was endorsed by the Inspector-General of Imperial Service Troops in these words:

"A most satisfactory report, and very, very creditable to Colonel Obaidullah Khan."

Reporting on the work of the signallers, the Inspector-General of Signalling wrote:

"The signallers have done extremely well, and great credit is due to the men themselves and to the Signalling Officer Jamadar Abdul Majid and his two Assistant Instructors. Both Colonel Obaidullah Khan and the officer commanding the regiment take a keen personal interest in the signalling efficiency of the corps, and the signallers are given every encouragement. The equipment is very complete and good, and is kept in most excellent order."

Both officers and men were greatly encouraged by these favourable reports. I am confident that, as time goes on, they will prove themselves more and more efficient. In the Imperial Service tests held this year, the Bhopal signallers stood second in the whole of India, and the signallers of the Janjira State were sent to Bhopal for instruction.

In the third year of my reign, I established an Advisory Council to consider and discuss matters relating to the general administration of the State. I found, however, that I was frequently faced with questions of a grave and confidential nature, which I could not place before this assembly. I, therefore, decided to create a second and smaller assembly for the consideration of such questions. The new council, called the Council of State, came into being in January 1908. It included, besides my two elder sons, the Muin-ul-muham, the Nasir-ul-muham, the Chief Secretary, and the Chief Accountant. My youngest son, Sahibzada Hamidullah Khan, was instructed to attend the meetings and listen to the discussions.

During the rainy season of this year, I received a letter from the Political Agent informing me that the Prince of Arcot, the head of an ancient and historic family in the Madras Presidency, desired to pay an informal visit to Bhopal, and requesting that arrangements might be made for his reception. The necessary orders were at once given to the Guest Department, and a guard of sowars was detailed to wait on him. The Prince arrived by mail train on 12th Rajab, 1326 A.H. (10th August, 1908). He was met at the railway station and welcomed on behalf of the State by Khan Bahadur Israr Hasan, the Nasir-ul-muham, who conducted him to the residence which had been prepared for him in the Hayat Afza garden. On the following day, accompanied by the same officer, he visited the principal sights of Bhopal, and at 3 o'clock in the afternoon called on me at the Sadar Manzil palace. He was escorted from the Hayat Afza garden by the Assistant Muin-ul-muham, and the Muin-ul-muham received him at the steps of the palace. The Prince is a man of refined manners and enlightened views. He exhibited a keen interest in the national movements of the Madras Presidency. He left Bhopal after a stay of two days.

CHAPTER III

A YEAR OF PROGRESS

IT had been decided that the quinquennial system of land settlement should terminate in the *fasli*[1] year 1315, by which time it was expected that the arrangements for the nineteen years' system, by which it was to be superseded, would be complete. Various circumstances, however, interfered with the progress of the work, and it was found necessary to extend the period of the quinquennial system for another year.

The new leases were distributed in all the districts between the 1st April and the 29th July of the year of 1909. The dates of issue and the names of the parties concerned had been previously notified in each *tahsil*, and on the days appointed the various *mustajirs* came to the Taj Mahal palace to receive their leases. These were distributed between 10 a.m. and 5 p.m., during

[1] *Fasli* (Arab. *fasl*=a season, crop) is the name applied to the solar era established in the reign of Akbar for revenue purposes. The *fasli* era was introduced to avoid the inconvenience of the *Hijra* calendar which, being lunar, does not correspond with the natural seasons. The *fasli* year 1315 commenced on April 2nd, 1907 A.D. (1326 A.H.).

which hours the Muin-ul-muham, and the Financial Secretary, were always in attendance, as well as the *nazims* of the three districts, the *tahsildars*, and the Receiver of State debts. The *mustajirs* were at the same time informed of the State dues outstanding against each village, and leases were granted only to those who agreed to discharge such arrears. The claims of *mustajirs* of long standing received the fullest consideration, the amounts due from their villages being materially reduced, or written off altogether. No securities or deposits were demanded from the lease holders, as the new system of collecting revenue, and the passing of the Land Revenue Act, rendered such precautions unnecessary.

On every lease that was issued I wrote with my own hand the words *Allahu Akbar*, "God is great," followed by *Bismillah-ir-Rahman-ir-Rahim*, "In the name of God, the Compassionate, the Merciful!"; and I also wrote on each the letter *suad* as a mark of my confirmation. Together with his lease, each lessee received from me a handful of grain. The custom of writing the words *Allahu Akbar* at the head of State documents is a very old one, dating probably from the reign of the Mogul Emperor Akbar. Whatever reasons Akbar may have had for using these words, it is purely as an act of homage to the Creator that they are used by the rulers of Bhopal. The words *Bismillah, etc.*, were added in my own time, in accordance with the Islamic belief that whatever is undertaken in the name of God will succeed. "Let every important act," said the Prophet, "be begun in the name of God, the Compassionate, the Merciful." The *mustajirs* considered it a happy omen to receive their leases and the grain from the hands of the Ruler, for they thought that this would bring a blessing on their labours, and cause their crops to be abundant. In the course of the distribution, arrears to the amount of Rs. 2,47,691 were recovered. The balance of the sum due was cancelled. Thus each village, as the new settlement came into operation, was relieved of its burden of debt. To every *mustajir* who paid the arrears due from his villages, or the amount fixed by me on reduction, I presented shawls and a medal, as a mark of my favour and approbation.

I am confident that, as time goes on, agricultural conditions will steadily improve; for the village lands, besides being unencumbered by debts, are, under the nineteen years' settlement, assessed at a very moderate rate. Only such lands are assessed as are actually under cultivation. Land lying fallow, or land that has never been cleared, is assessed at a very low rate; so that it pays both the cultivator and the *mustajir* to bring such areas under cultivation. The various kinds of *siwai* lands, which were formerly under the control of the Forest Department, and were put up to auction every year, have now been included in the areas farmed out to *mustajirs*, and their boundaries have been demarcated accordingly. This and similar measures, together with the rights conferred on tenants and *mustajirs* by the new Land Revenue Act, have contributed much to the success of the nineteen years' settlement. In every village where a *mustajir* had acquired *sir* (proprietary) rights, but failed to obtain a renewal of his lease under the new settlement, it was laid down that he could not be deprived of such rights, and that the new *mustajir* had no power to eject him from his holding.

The announcement of the various concessions to be granted under the new system both to tenants and to *mustajirs,* and of the moderate rates at which lands were to be assessed, created so favourable an impression that in almost all the villages there was competition for the leases, three, four, and in some cases an even larger number of applications being received.

The only portions of the State which were not brought under the new system were certain villages in the Diwangang *tahsil,* which had already been settled on the *ryatwari* system for a period of 17 years, and certain others where a thirty years' settlement had been introduced by Maulavi Abdul Jabbar Khan, at the time when he held the office of Wazir.

In times of illness we need not only good doctors and medicines, but good nursing. I know from my own experience how much patients suffer in this country in consequence of the ignorance which prevails of the art of nursing. In Europe many women receive expert training in this art, which they practise as a profession. They are ready for service not only in hospitals and nursing homes, but in private houses; and as they study other arts, and acquire many other accomplishments besides that of ministering to the sick, they are frequently employed in families where they combine the duties of nurse and governess. There is scarcely a woman in Europe who does not possess some knowledge of nursing; and ladies of the highest position often undergo courses of training in hospitals, and are as eager to become efficient nurses as if their livings depended upon it. In India, unhappily, the reverse is the case. Owing to the backward state of female education, and the absence of training institutions, Indian women seldom possess even a rudimentary knowledge of the duties of a nurse. Of first aid to the sick they know nothing, and they are consequently helpless in cases of accident or sudden illness.

Steps to remedy this state of affairs have not been lacking; and it is now no longer impossible, thanks to the efforts of Lady Minto and her predecessors, to obtain the services of a trained nurse. But it is, as yet, only the ruling Chiefs and the rich who have been benefited; for even ordinary well-to-do people, to say nothing of the humbler classes, are unable to pay the high fees charged by trained European nurses. Moreover, these nurses are seldom willing to stay more than a few days in an Indian house, where the mode of life is so little suited to them. It is surely, therefore, a matter of the utmost importance that steps should be taken to train Indian women as nurses, so that people in every grade of society may be able to obtain the assistance they so urgently need.

It was with these thoughts in my mind that I determined to establish a School for nursing in Bhopal. As Her Excellency Lady Minto had done so much for the cause of nursing in India, I asked and obtained Her Excellency's permission to name the institution after her. I called it, accordingly, The Lady Minto Nursing School, and a start was made on a small scale in the month of August, 1909.

As this kind of education was quite new to the people of Bhopal, it was no easy matter to find pupils for the new school. All kinds of objections and excuses were made; but at length, by dint of persuasion, the promise of scholarships, and a little gentle pressure, a class of girls between the ages of 10 and 12 was got together, and work was commenced. Instruction was imparted both in Urdu and in English. I made the school a branch of the Lansdowne Hospital, and placed it under the management of Mrs. Barnes, the lady doctor.

I also took advantage of Mrs. Barnes' appointment to open a class for instruction in midwifery. It would be difficult to exaggerate the sufferings which Indian women have frequently to endure at the hands of inexperienced *dais*. Many are the cases in which death, or a life-long disablement, has resulted from ignorance, or some act of carelessness, on the part of these ill-qualified practitioners. It is at times of child-birth, and for the treatment of the various ailments peculiar to the female sex, that qualified Indian attendants are so urgently needed. I had always been desirous that the State should provide instruction in this branch of nursing, and my desire had increased with the steady rise in the birth-rate which, at the time of which I am writing, had reached an average of twenty births a day. I first took the matter in hand in the year 1909 ; but the departure of Miss Blong, who up till then had held the post of Lady Doctor, necessitated the postponement of my plans, for I knew that it would be useless to open a class until I had secured the services of a thoroughly competent and sympathetic teacher. Miss Blong was succeeded by Miss Earl ; but from what I was able to gather of the latter lady's temperament, it seemed to me that I could not expect from her the ready co-operation on which the success of my scheme depended. The next to hold the office was Mrs. Barnes. In addition to discharging her duties in a highly efficient manner, Mrs. Barnes showed herself to be obedient, full of energy, and kind-hearted ; and I felt that she would devote herself with enthusiasm to the carrying out of my wishes.

I accordingly called together all the midwives in Bhopal—the profession is confined to certain families in which it has become hereditary—and ordered them to attend daily at the hospital to receive instruction from Mrs. Barnes in the duties of their calling. I also gave orders that they were to send their daughters to Mrs. Barnes for elementary training, in order that they might start at the very beginning, and be taken through a complete course of midwifery. It was found impossible to proceed thus with the older women, and to these oral instruction only was given. A certificate was granted to every woman whom the Lady Doctor considered competent to undertake maternity cases ; and I issued an order that only those who obtained such certificates were to practise as midwives, and that any woman contravening this order would be punished. Persons requiring the services of a midwife were advised to make application to the Lady Doctor, who would see that they were suitably supplied. These orders had very satisfactory results. Many applications were received by the Lady Doctor, while the midwives themselves began to exercise much greater care in the performance of their duties. In order to make my scheme popular I directed that every woman who attended the classes should receive an allowance of five rupees a month. Mrs. Barnes proved herself a most efficient and sympathetic teacher, and under her management the classes grew so large that it became necessary to provide her with an assistant. I selected Miss Waller, an M.D. of America, for this post. I trust that this school may not only be of permanent benefit to the women of Bhopal, but may serve as a model for similar institutions elsewhere. In any State or Province, a system of medical relief which does not include the provision of trained nurses and midwives can benefit only half the population, since it leaves out of account the needs of the female sex.

There is no doubt that our minds are developed and our manners improved by good company and pleasant surroundings. Social intercourse widens our outlook on life, and thereby helps us to attain a higher state of civilization. Societies and clubs for ladies have long been a feature of the social life of England, and English women derive much pleasure and benefit from these institutions. But Indian women unhappily possess few such advantages ; and when I thought of the idle superstitions and foolish customs which occupied the time and the minds of so many even of our better-class women, and how their daughters and grand-daughters are growing up in the same darkened atmosphere, I felt how needful it was that something should be done to bring light and new ideas into their minds, and new interests into their lives. After giving much thought to these matters, I came to the conclusion that, as female education had already made some progress in Bhopal, much benefit might result, especially to the rising generation of girls, by the establishment of some kind of social club, provided that this could be done without detriment to the studies of those whose education was still in progress. In putting this idea into execution I was prompted by the desire to help not only my own people, but my sisters throughout India. It was my hope that the Bhopal Ladies' Club would lead to the establishment of similar institutions in other States, and in British India ; for throughout the entire country there is not, so far as I know, or there was not at the time of which I write, a single club designed for the use of *parda-nashin* ladies.

I decided that the club should at first be confined to the ladies of my own family, and the wives and female relatives of the gentry and officers of the State ; and that girls studying in the various schools should be received as visitors on special occasions. I knew that before my scheme could be successfully launched, a good deal of prejudice would have to be overcome, and that I must curb my impatience and proceed slowly and cautiously. As a preliminary step, I consulted the ladies of my own family who one and all enthusiastically welcomed my proposal, and expressed their willingness to become members of the club. After this, I called a meeting of all the ladies I considered eligible for membership, at which I explained the nature and aims of a ladies' club, and announced my intention of establishing one in Bhopal.

It was at this time, namely in the year 1909, that their Royal Highnesses The Prince and Princess of Wales visited India, and I had the proud privilege of an audience with Her Royal Highness, now Queen Mary, at Indore. As an expression of my gratitude for the kind and honourable reception that was accorded me on this occasion, I decided to set up some kind of memorial to Her Royal Highness in the capital of my State; and it seemed to me that nothing could serve better to perpetuate Her Royal Highness's memory than the association of her name with the club I was about to establish. I felt at the same time that no name could be more appropriate than that of this gracious lady for an institution that aimed at bringing culture and refinement into the lives of the women of India.

Before the end of the year, the Princess of Wales Club was an accomplished fact. I accepted the position of Patroness, and Aftab Begam, the niece of the late Nawab Ihtisham-ud-daula, who had been educated under my personal supervision, was elected Secretary. Rules and regulations were drawn up, and it was decided that European and Anglo-Indian ladies should be eligible for membership. The club was located in the Ali Manzil, a beautiful building standing in an extensive garden surrounded by high walls. Furniture, books, periodicals, and the materials for indoor and outdoor games suitable for women, were supplied by the State. This made it possible to keep the entrance fee and subscription very low. The rules laid down that, from time to time, lectures should be given, or papers read, by members of the club on subjects of feminine interest; and to stimulate enthusiasm in this feature of the club, I myself took the lead, and read the first paper. The Princess of Wales Club has already done much for the women of Bhopal; and I hope that, with the blessing of the Almighty, the light which has been kindled will grow brighter and brighter, and that its rays may spread throughout the Mussalman community.

Another institution founded this year was the King Edward Museum. The handsome building of red sand-stone set apart for this purpose was originally intended for the Alexandra High School; but for various reasons this idea had been abandoned, and the school was located in a building erected in my mother's reign, and known as Benazir. I called the institution the King Edward Museum in memory of His late Majesty, King Edward VII, for whom the people of Bhopal had always entertained the deepest respect and affection.

A museum is a necessary adjunct to an up-to-date educational system. It provides both instruction and intelligent amusement. It enables us to take an interest in, and to study the arts and industries of our own country, and to compare them with those of other countries and other times, and affords many other opportunities for self-education.

I had always intended to establish a museum in Bhopal ; and as my people were now sufficiently educated to appreciate its advantages, I decided that the time had come to put my plan into execution. I pushed forward my preparations as rapidly as possible, as I proposed to ask His Excellency the Viceroy, who was expected to visit Bhopal in the latter part of the year, to perform the opening ceremony, and I was anxious that everything should be in readiness before His Excellency's arrival. The work was carried out under the supervision of my eldest son, Nawab Nasrullah Khan, assisted by Maulavi Nasir-ud-din, and such was the energy they displayed that not only was the building ready to be opened on the day appointed, but many interesting exhibits had been collected and placed on view. The grounds surrounding the Museum were planted with trees and shrubs, and a portion was walled in and made into a pleasure-garden, or retreat, where purdah ladies could rest and take the air.

Edward Museum, Bhopal.

CHAPTER IV

LORD MINTO AT BHOPAL

TOWARDS the end of January, 1909, I was informed by Col. Hugh Daly, the Agent to the Governor-General in Central India, that His Excellency Lord Minto had expressed his intention of visiting Bhopal, and that I might expect his arrival in the month of November. This intelligence gave me immense pleasure, for I had not yet had the honour of welcoming the representative of the King-Emperor to my capital.

The visits which a Viceroy pays to protected States do much to promote friendly relations between Indian Princes and the paramount power, and are productive of many other results advantageous to both parties. A Ruler of a protected State looks upon the visit of a Viceroy as a personal honour. In Lord Minto's case the honour was felt to be exceptionally great; for no Viceroy ever established happier relations with the ruling Chiefs and their families, while the period of his administration stands out as one of the most important and momentous in the history of modern India. In addition to these feelings, which I shared with other Rulers, I felt a special pride in welcoming to my State a descendant of the famous Earl of Minto who had governed India in the early part of the last century, and who during those stormy days had shown himself a true friend to the Rulers of Bhopal. My readers can, therefore, imagine my elation on hearing of His Excellency's advent, and my desire to prepare a welcome worthy of so distinguished a guest.

Anxious though I was that His Excellency should be received and entertained with becoming state, I did not fail to consider how the occasion could best be turned to practical account. I have always grudged the money that is spent on extravagant displays of grandeur. I hold that the permanent improvement of a town or a building is a far greater compliment to a visitor than its temporary adornment; and though the city of Bhopal was gaily decorated, and no expense was spared to do honour to His Excellency's visit, I endeavoured, as far as the very special nature of the occasion permitted, to keep this principle in view throughout my preparations.

I lost no time in issuing orders for the reception and entertainment of my guests An extensive and elaborate camp for the accommodation of Lord Minto and his party was laid out in the grounds of the Lal Kothi, and everything was done to ensure the comfort and convenience of the European and other friends whom I was inviting to Bhopal to meet His Excellency.

A number of old and dilapidated houses abutting

on the roads which led from the railway station to the Lal Kothi, and to Ahmedabad, were either repaired or pulled down, the owners in the latter case receiving compensation. This greatly improved the appearance of the city, and was also very beneficial from a sanitary point of view. The road from the railway station to the Pul Pukhta was decorated with festoons of leaves and flowers suspended from tall bamboos, and at frequent intervals triumphal arches were erected, In the city every street was gay with flags and bunting. Many people decorated their houses, and all along the route which the Viceregal procession was to follow, stands were erected for spectators, and tastefully adorned with pictures flowers, and evergreens. As a result of the combined efforts of the State and the populace, the city of Bhopal wore an air oi radiant festivity.

The camp for His Excellency's staff was also located in the grounds of the Lal Kothi, and my other guests were lodged in the Guest House, and in a camp laid out in the garden adjoining it. Both these camps were gay with flower-beds, and at night were lit with electric light. A scheme for lighting the city of Bhopal by electricity had already received my sanction. I pushed the scheme forward as rapidly as possible when I received notice of His Excellency's visit, and by the month of October, the illumination of the main roads to the Lal Kothi and Ahmedabad was completed. The catering arrangements for the

Viceregal party and my other European guests were carried out by Mr. Peliti of Simla, while my Indian guests were provided for by the State guest department. My Chief Secretary and Military Secretary were specially deputed to attend to the needs of all the guests, and an enquiry office was opened in each camp.

A detailed programme of the arrangements for His Excellency's visit was prepared, and every officer was carefully instructed as to the duties he was to perform. In view of the recent activities of mischievous and disloyal people in British India, the strictest watch was kept on the movements of all unknown persons. This was done under the supervision and direction of Khan Bahadur Israr Hasan Khan, the Nasir-ul-muham. Every quarter of the city, and the roads leading thereto, were patrolled night and day by police officers in plain clothes, and each camp was surrounded by a cordon of police or troops, and none was allowed to enter without a pass signed by the Nasir-ul-muham. These cordons were under the personal orders of Colonel Obaidullah Khan, Commander-in-Chief of the forces of the State, who exercised a general supervision over the precautionary measures. These preparations were inspected before His Excellency's arrival by two officers of the Government of India, who expressed their complete satisfaction with the arrangements that had been made.

By the evening of the 9th November, all my

visitors, with the exception of the Viceregal party, had arrived in Bhopal, as had also the Chiefs of the Bhopal Agency who had come, at the invitation of the Political Agent, to pay their respects to the Viceroy. These, with their staffs and retinues, were guests of the State. His Excellency's arrival took place the following morning. From an early hour, great crowds of spectators assembled along the route to the railway station, which was lined on either side by troops and police. A guard of honour was drawn up outside the station, and on the platform, which had been profusely decorated, seats were arranged in three blocks for the Sardars of the State. These were assigned places according to their rank, and orders were issued that their costumes were to be, as far as possible, of a uniform character. I reached the station accompanied by my three sons, the Muin-ul-muham, and the Nasir-ul-muham, at 7-55 a.m. The Sirdars and State officials were already in their places. Those who had been invited to attend were Mian Yasin Muhammad Khan ; Mian Yar Muhammad Khan ; Mian Aqil Muhammad Khan ; Syad Zamir-ud-din, Chief Secretary; Munshi Abdur Rauf Khan, State Vakil ; Mian Iqbal Muhammad Khan ; Bakhshi Faridullah Khan ; Badshah Syad Abdul Aziz, Sardar Bahadur ; Major Abdul Qaiyum Khan ; Captain Abdul Hasan Khan : Captain Abdul Wahid ; Major Mirza Muhammad Beg, Sardar Bahadur ; Lieutenant Muhammad Ibrahim ; Mr. Sakhawat

Husain, Private Secretary; Munshi Mansab Ali, Financial Secretary; Munshi Abdus Samad, Military Secretary; Munshi Oudh Narayan Bisarata, Chief Accountant; Qari Muhammad Sulaiman, Director of Public Instruction; Khan Sahib Afzur Rahim, Director of Land Records; Mr. Jamshedji, Assistant Nasir-ul-muham; Maulavi Fasli Rab, Settlement Officer; Munshi Syad Qudrat Ali, President of the Municipality; Seth Narayan Das, Treasury Officer; Dr. Abdur Rahman, Assistant Surgeon; Mufti Anwarul Haqq, Assistant Chief Secretary; Mr. Muhammad Sulaiman, Sessions Judge; Maulavi Abdul Ghafur, Officer of the Legislative Department; Mr. Majid Husain, Officer in charge of the *deorhi* of Nawab Nasrullah Khan; and Munshi Amir Ahmad, Private Secretary to Colonel Obaidullah Khan.

The Viceregal train entered the station at 8 a.m., and His Excellency's arrival was announced by a salute of 31 guns. Accompanied by the Agent to the Governor-General in Central India, and the Political Agent in Bhopal, I met His Excellency as he descended from his saloon, and was formally introduced by the Agent to the Governor-General. The Political Agent then presented Nawab Nasrullah Khan, Colonel Obaidullah Khan, Sahibzada Hamidullah Khan, the Muin-ul-muham, the Nasir-ul-muham, Mr. Payne, and Mr. Austin Cook. Her Excellency the Countess of Minto next alighted; and after I had been introduced to her, The

Viceroy, attended by Colonel Obaidullah Khan, the Political Agent, and the members of his staff, inspected the guard-of-honour. With a thoughtfulness for the comfort of others, which even on ceremonial occasions he never failed to display, Lord Minto begged me to keep my seat while the inspection took place. The Sardars of the State were presented to the Countess of Minto during the interval thus provided.

These ceremonies being concluded, I took my seat beside His Excellency in the State coach, and we led the procession to the Lal Kothi. The Political Agent and an Aide-de-Camp came with us. In the carriage which immediately followed were the Countess of Minto, the Agent to the Governor-General, Nawab Nasrullah Khan, and His Excellency's Military Secretary. The third carriage contained Lady Eileen Elliot, Lady Antrim, Sahibzada Hamidullah Khan, and the First Assistant to the Agent to the Governor-General. The remaining guests and Sardars followed in order of precedence in other carriages.

His Excellency greatly admired the decorations, and was much pleased by the enthusiastic welcome of the crowds that had collected to witness his arrival. On reaching the Pul Pukhta, he was greeted by the students of the Sulaimania and Jahangiria schools who were assembled at this point. The students were dressed in the uniforms of their respective schools, and each carried a flag on which the arms of the State were represented. As the State coach passed them they lowered their flags and gave a hearty cheer, His Excellency was much touched by this incident, and made many enquiries about the students and their schools. The Lal Kothi was reached in twenty minutes. I remained in conversation with their Excellencies for a few moments, and then returned to the Sadar Manzil palace.

At 10 o'clock, I sent Sahibzada Hamidullah Khan and Munshi Israr Hasan Khan to enquire after their Excellencies' welfare on my behalf. They were conducted to the drawing-room of the Lal Kothi, where they were received at the edge of the carpet by the Foreign Secretary and the Military Secretary. The Foreign Secretary presented them with *attar* and *pan*, and when they rose to take leave he accompanied them as far as the edge of the carpet. At 10-45 o'clock some officers of the viceregal staff came to escort me to the Lal Kothi for the purpose of paying my State visit, and ten minutes later I set out from the Sadar Manzil, accompanied by Nawab Nasrullah Khan, Sahibzada Hamidullah Khan, the Muin-ul-muham, the Nasir-ul-muham, Sardar Bahadur Abdul Aziz Badshah, and Mian Iqbal Muhammad Khan. Colonel Obaidullah Khan was A.-D.-C. to His Excellency, and was therefore on duty at the Lal Kothi. The visit took place in a *shamiana* erected in the grounds, and a guard-of-honour was provided by the 56th Punjabi Rifles, at that time stationed at Sehore. I was met on my arrival by the Foreign Secretary, and when I entered the *shamiana,* His Excellency advanced to the edge of the carpet to receive me. He then led me to a chair on the right of his own, showing me much courtesy. We conversed together for some minutes, after which the Sardars, who were seated on His Excellency's left, presented their *nazarana,* the Political Agent announcing the name of each as he came forward. Before my departure His Excellency garlanded me, and presented me with *attar* and *pan,* the same being presented to the Sardars by the Military Secretary. The ceremonial portion of my visit concluded, I walked across to the Lal Kothi and called on the Countess of Minto.

At 12-20 p.m. the Muin-ul-muham, Mian Aqil Muhammad Khan, and Sardar Bahadur Major Mirza Karim Beg, waited on His Excellency at the Lal Kothi, to escort him to the Sadar Manzil, where the return visit was to be paid. It had been arranged that the Countess of Minto should return my call at 1-15, after the State visit had taken place. I was informed, however, that Her Excellency and other ladies of the viceregal party had expressed a great desire to witness the reception of the representative of the King-Emperor by an Indian ruler of their own sex. I accordingly despatched a second deputation to the Lal Kothi, the first having already set out, and the ladies were brought in motor cars to the palace, where they watched the proceedings from a gallery overlooking the durbar hall.

The Viceroy, accompanied by his staff, and escorted by a detachment of the Bhopal Imperial Service cavalry, reached the Sadar Manzil a few minutes before one o'clock. As his carriage entered the courtyard, the guard-of-honour, posted in front of the main entrance to the palace, presented arms, and a salute of 31 guns was fired from the fort. Supported by my two sons, Nawab Nasrullah Khan and Sahibzada Hamidullah Khan, I received His Excellency as he alighted, and conducted him to the durbar hall. We took our seats on two gilded chairs placed in the centre of the hall on a dais covered with cloth of gold, while the members of His Excellency's staff, amongst whom was my son Colonel Obaidullah Khan, sat on the right side of the dais, and the State Sardars in order of rank on the left. All those who took part in the reception at the railway station were present at the durbar.

As is customary on such occasions the proceedings were brief, and of a purely formal character. After the usual exchange of courtesies, the leading nobles and officials, twelve in number, presented *nazarana*. This was followed by the distribution of *attar* and *pan* and garlands. I myself garlanded and offered *attar* and *pan* to His Excellency, and also to the Agent to the Governor-General and the Political Agent. The members of the Viceregal staff were garlanded by Nawab Nasrullah Khan, and the Sardars by the Keeper of the *toshakhana*. The durbar was then at an end,

The Earl of Minto.

and His Excellency returned to the Lal Kothi. As soon as he had departed, I had the pleasure of receiving Her Excellency Lady Minto and the ladies who accompanied her. There were with me at this time my three daughters-in-law, the Qaisar Dulhan Sahiba, the Shahriar Dulhan Sahiba and Shah Bano Begam Sahiba, and my five grandchildren, Sahibzadi Birjis Jahan Begam, Sahibzada Muhammad Rafiqullah Khan, Sahibzada Muhammad Habibullah Khan, Sahibzada Wahid-uz-zafar Khan, and Sahibzada Muhammad Syad-uz-zafar Khan.

At four o'clock in the afternoon, a military gymkhana was held on the parade ground, and was witnessed by the viceregal party and all my other guests, both European and Indian. I took with me on this occasion four of my little grandsons, dressed as soldiers. Their uniforms suited them extremely well, and everybody complimented me on the smart appearance of my bodyguard. The programme, which had been arranged by the Military Department, was commenced as soon as their Excellencies arrived on the ground. After a number of keenly-contested competitions, there was a realistic sham-fight, which was watched by the spectators with great interest. From a hill on the south of the parade ground a body of tribesmen opened fire on a British force, and then advanced to the attack. They were quickly and cleverly surrounded by the British troops, and many of them were declared to be killed and the remainder captured. The wounded tribesmen were carried past our tents by their captors. A grand march past, and the distribution of prizes, at which Lady Minto was kind enough to preside, brought the programme to an end.

CHAPTER V

SOME CEREMONIES AND A BANQUET

THE next morning at seven o'clock, Lady Minto visited the Lansdowne Hospital. I accompanied her with Birjis Jahan Begam. From the hospital we proceeded to the Sultania Girls' School. Here we were joined by Lady Eileen Elliot and Lady Antrim. At the entrance to the building, which had been decorated very beautifully, we were received by Mrs. Bakhsh, the Lady Superintendent, and the members of the teaching staff. The students, all uniformly dressed, were assembled in the large school-room to welcome us. As we entered the room they rose to their feet and saluted; and when we had taken our seats they sang the national anthem, after which several girls recited poems, some in Urdu, and some in English. The recitations were listened to with much interest, while every one spoke in high terms of the behaviour and discipline of the students. Mrs. Bakhsh read an address giving an account of the work done in the school, and the progress that had been made. The address was then placed in a casket and presented to Lady Minto, who rose and replied as follows :—

"Your Highness and Ladies,

I am deeply touched by your remarks regarding the pleasure caused by His Excellency's and my visit to Bhopal, and also by the importance you attach to my visit to the Sultania Girls' School. In no State in India should the condition of its female population be so well considered as here in Bhopal, having had, as it has had, a succession of four female Rulers. Under such unique circumstances it is peculiarly fitting that the womanly heart of the Ruler of Bhopal should turn in sympathy to female education. The influence of women is as great, as vast, and as beneficial in India as it is in the western hemisphere. All over the world it is the mothers who have influenced past generations, and who will still exert that influence over the generations of the present and the future. But it must be remembered that in order to maintain a healthy influence, the women of all nations must be in sympathy and in touch with the times. I have often heard of Your Highness's endeavours to promote the cause of female education in your State, and I strongly agree with the sentiments which Mrs. Bakhsh has just uttered regarding Your Highness's wise attitude in strictly respecting the *parda* system, although in many ways this system may have its disadvantages. No real progress can be made if ancient customs are rudely broken in contradiction to the wishes of those by whom that progress is most desired. I am glad to hear that the character of the education given here is of a highly practical nature, and I am glad also to notice that the list of subjects taught is headed by that of religious instruction.

At present female education in India is in its infancy, but the strides that it has made during the last few years is enormous. Up to now, European models have been taken for text-books and subjects ; but I have no doubt that before long Indian ladies will write their own text-books and strike out with their own ideas, borrowing the experience and accumulated wisdom of the West to quicken the experience and inherited traditions of the East. I consider that the growth in your numbers is a most happy augury, and I trust that it will continue in the future. Before closing I should like to quote to you a few words spoken by Sir Charles Wood, who was afterwards Lord Hallifax, which I think are particularly appropriate to the present occasion: "By female education a far greater proportional impulse is imparted to the educational and moral tone of a people than by the education of men." These words are very true, as, with a nation as domesticated as the peoples of India, the mother and wife wield real power. If their development is allowed to lag behind that of the men, the country cannot progress. I again thank you for the reception you have given me here to-day, and I wish this institution all success."

At the close of her speech, Her Excellency distributed the Prizes which had been awarded to successful students; and before leaving the School she was kind enough to write the following remarks in the visitors' book:—

"I was greatly interested in my visit to the Sultania Girls' School. The pupils gave an excellent English recitation, and their brightness and intelligence were very evident.

The interest Her Highness takes in the School must be of the greatest assistance to both teachers and pupils, and it gave me much pleasure to hear what marked improvement was being made in the education of the children."

Our next destination was the Princess of Wales Club, which Her Excellency had kindly consented to open. The club building had been artistically decorated by Miss Atia Fyzi and Abru Begam. On arrival Her Excellency was received by eight ladies of my family, amongst whom were my three daughters-in-law. The assembled members stood up as we entered the club, and, when we had taken our seats, an address of welcome was read by the Secretary, Aftab Begam, after which I handed a golden key to Her Excellency, and requested her to open the club. On receiving the key, she rose, and said:

"YOUR HIGHNESS AND LADIES,

It is with the greatest pleasure that I have heard the remarks just made by Aftab Begam, the Secretary of this Club. I consider that the idea of having a ladies' club here in Bhopal is a striking illustration of the progress that is being made in the State. Such institutions have not existed for so very long in England, and the fact that this club is now being started here shows how thoroughly Your Highness appreciates the importance of moving with the times. After school-days are over, one's further education is obtained by conversing and mingling with others, and no place could be better suited to this purpose than an institution such as this. Her Royal Highness the Princess of Wales will, I am sure, be deeply interested to know that her memory is being perpetuated in the formation of this Ladies' Club, and I trust that it will add brightness and new interest to the social life of the ladies of Bhopal. I can offer no better advice to the members than to imitate in their lives and works the Princess of Wales and also the Begam. I have much pleasure in declaring this Club open, and in wishing all success to it and its members."

This speech having been translated into English by Miss Atia Fyzi, Her Excellency declared the Club open, after which all the members were presented to her. As she was about to depart, she was told that the girls of the Victoria School had come into the club garden to make their salams to her. She at once said that she would go to them ; so I led her into the garden, where she graciously received their greetings, which they accompanied with showers of flowers. We had now reached the end of our programme, and Lady Minto returned to the Lal Kothi, having devoted the entire morning to the interests of the women of Bhopal.

In the afternoon, His Excellency opened the new set of class-rooms which had been added to the Alexandra High School. I reached the school a few minutes before half past four, the hour fixed for the ceremony. On arrival, Their Excellencies were welcomed by Mr. Payne, the Principal of the School, and the members of the teaching staff, while I received them as they entered the large hall in which the students and a distinguished company of visitors were assembled. Amongst the latter were the Raja Sahib of Rajgarh, the Raja Sahib of Narsingarh, and many of the Sardars of the State, whose sons were being educated in the school.

The proceedings commenced with the reading and presentation of an address by the Principal. On receiving the casket containing the address, His Excellency rose and said :

"MR. PAYNE,

I thank you for the address you have presented to me as Principal of the Alexandra High School, and I hope you will express to your staff and the students my sincere appreciation of the hearty welcome they have given to Lady Minto and myself. It is a great pleasure to both of us to be here and to take our share in inaugurating one of the many useful institutions Her Highness has bestowed on Bhopal. Bhopal owes much to Her Highness's enlightened wisdom. Her Highness foresees the vast importance of awakening the upper classes of her State to a sense of the responsibilities which it is their duty to undertake, whilst providing at the same time for the general training of her subjects for the public service. She hopes in the future to look to her own subjects to assist her in her administration. She hopes to fill the chief positions in her State service from amongst them, and not from the outside world. And with this view, the Alexandra School aims, as you have told me, at being something more than an ordinary High School. It will indeed, supply the teaching obtainable at other schools, but will, in addition to that, encourage amongst its pupils the many qualities that go to form that strength of character so invaluable in the battles of every-day life. It is the discipline of early life which goes so far to make the man. The famous Persian poet, Sadi, very truly said: "The severity of the tutor is more useful than the indulgence of the father." I do not doubt that, as years go on, the manly training of the Alexandra High School will prove the truth of the poet's words. I hope that the pupils who leave these walls will grow up happy, healthy, and God-fearing subjects, loyal and devoted to Her Highness, the distinguished administrator, to whom they are so much indebted.

Your Highness, Ladies and Gentlemen, I now declare the Alexandra High School to be open."

His Excellency's speech was followed by the opening ceremony, after which the students entertained the company with recitations. A beautiful English poem recited by Sahibzada Hamidullah Khan was warmly applauded.

Before the meeting dispersed, about twenty students received prizes for meritorious work. These were presented by Lady Minto.

From the school we all made our way to the King Edward Museum, which was also to be opened that afternoon. Here the honours were done by Nawab Nasrullah Khan and the Muin-ul-muham. The latter having read a short report of the work already done in connection with the Museum, the Viceroy rose and made the following speech :

MR. NASIR-UD-DIN,"

I am very glad that Her Highness has done me the honour of asking me to open this Museum, and may I say too that I am well aware of the labour you have devoted to its inauguration, and the energy with which Nawab Nasrullah Khan has furthered the object which Her Highness has in view. The importance of Museums is becoming more and more recognised. They are not only places for sight-seers, but should play a prominent part in placing within the reach of the people the object-lessons which should do much to encourage and interest them in that scientific and technical training which is one of the great needs of the present day. It is every day becoming more evident to the leading minds of India that the benefits of mere literary teaching are limited, and that more practical methods of instruction are necessary to meet the demand for employment, upon the supply of which the contentment of the people must so largely depend. I feel sure that this Museum, under the watchful care of Her Highness, will be administered on well-thought-out lines, and that it will afford many facilities for the development of agriculture, forestry, mineralogy, and the Arts. I hope that the boys of the Alexandra School, which I have just opened, will often frequent it. I trust that it will prove an institution worthy of the great King-Emperor whose name it bears, and that it will fulfil all the hopes and intentions with which Her Highness has so generously founded it."

At the conclusion of his speech, His Excellency declared the Museum open. The assembly then broke up, and, after some time had been spent in viewing the exhibits, His Excellency returned to the Lal Kothi, and the guests to their camp.

In the evening there was a State banquet at the Rahat Manzil. The palace and the surrounding gardens, as well as the entire length of the road from the Lal Kothi to Ahmedabad, were brilliantly illuminated. The city walls, the Fort, the Qasr-i-sultani, and many other buildings, were ablaze with countless coloured lights, and even the neighbouring hills were illuminated. It was a fairy-like and fascinating spectacle, and one that will long be remembered by those who witnessed it.

Their Excellencies reached the palace at eight o'clock, by which time all the other guests were assembled. According to my usual custom, I entered the banqueting-hall as dessert was being served. My three sons, and the Revenue and Judicial Ministers accompanied me. After the royal toasts had been honoured, I proposed the health of Their Excellencies in the following words:

"YOUR EXCELLENCIES, LADIES AND GENTLEMEN,

I cannot find words to express the sincere and heartfelt pleasure which the visit of Your Excellency and Lady Minto to Bhopal has given me. During the reign of my revered mother, Your Excellency's predecessors, on more than one occasion, conferred a similar honour on the State, but this is the first time that I, myself, have had the privilege of welcoming to my territories the representative of His Imperial Majesty the King-Emperor. My joy on this occasion has been enhanced by what I cannot but regard as a very happy coincidence. It was in the beginning of the nineteenth century that the State of Bhopal, under the rule of my ancestor Nawab Wazir Muhammad Khan, was engaged in a deadly struggle with the combined forces of Gwalior and the Bhonsla Raja. At that critical time, Your Excellency's great-grand-father was Governor-General of British India, and it was through the wise policy which he then advocated that the way was paved for the treaty which brought Bhopal under the protection of the British Government, and which laid the foundation of that loyalty to the ruling power for which the State has ever since been famous. It was the *kharita* of Your Excellency's ancestor despatched on the 7th January, 1810, which sowed the seed of that peace and prosperity which the State has for so many years enjoyed. I look upon it as a most happy omen, that Your Excellency's visit has practically coincided with the centenary of that memorable event: and I regard myself as doubly honoured, in that I am privileged to entertain one who is at once the Viceroy of His Majesty the King-Emperor and a descendant of one of the greatest benefactors of my State.

Your Excellency, I am confident, needs no assurances from me of devotion to and friendship towards the British Government. I belong to a family whose unswerving loyalty has never, from the day when it first rose to power, been called in question: a family that was the first among all the ruling families of India to pay honour to the British flag, and the first to offer its friendship to the British Power. A perusal of the history of Bhopal, and more especially of the reigns of my grandmother, Nawab Sikandar Begam, and my mother, Nawab Shah Jahan Begam, will show that since the government of the State has been in female hands its loyalty has been more and more manifest. That I, who come last, may maintain unsullied the honour of the Begams of Bhopal is my dearest ambition, that those who come after me may regard its preservation as their most sacred duty is my constant prayer.

Your Excellency, I thank God that the loyalty of my family is fully reflected in the hearts of my subjects; indeed it is difficult for us who live in Bhopal to realise that such a thing as disloyalty exists. England has won her way to greatness, not by the force of arms, but by her moral strength, and it is this moral strength which compels the admiration and fealty of every right-minded person. It was, indeed, well for India that she came under control of such a power—a control which has given to her people the inestimable gifts of peace, justice and liberty, and which has led to a period of prosperity and progress, the like of which had never before been dreamt of. It is beyond dispute that the vast majority of His Majesty's Indian subjects, and especially the Muhammadan section of them, gratefully acknowledge the manifold blessings that have accrued to them under British rule, the permanency of which they regard as the only guarantee of their welfare. The disloyalty of the few only serves to emphasize the loyalty of the many. As I have already said, we in Bhopal have little acquaintance with this minority; for my own part, those who compose it remind me of nothing so much as of Sadi's bat, who, happening to open his eyes in the day-light, and finding he could not see, straightway fell to abusing the sun. Speaking as a Muhammadan, I can say without fear of contradiction, that the loyalty of my co-religionists to the British government is inspired by no transitory or worldly interests, but is founded on the teaching of their Holy Book, in which it is written, "Verily thou wilt find the nearest friends of the believers amongst those who call themselves Christians because they have priests and monks, and they are not proud."

I have no hesitation in saying, and I know that every Ruling Chief will endorses my words, that it is the wise and broad-minded policy initiated by Your Excellency that has, like the sun that brightens the earth, dispersed the clouds that were gathering over our country. As a skilful captain navigates his ship safely through the perils of a hurricane Your Excellency has delivered India from a great calamity; and thus for the second time in history her peoples, and the people of Bhopal in particular, are indebted to those statesmanlike qualities which are hereditary in Your Excellency's family.

I do not intend to weary you by speaking of the administrative difficulties that I have had to face during the eight years of my reign, for these are matters with which Your Excellency's government is already acquainted. One thing only I would like to say in this connection, which is, that the abolition of the office of Prime Minister, and the creation in its place of the two offices of Revenue Minister and Judicial Minister, the first of my important reforms, has proved most beneficial to the State, and has greatly facilitated the work of administration. I have received much assistance from these two officers, and also from my eldest son, Nawab Nasrullah Khan, who has carried out in a most efficient manner the various duties that have been entrusted to him. I desire also to offer my thanks to the Hon'ble Colonel Daly and to Major Bayley for the help and advice they have at all times been ready to place at my disposal.

Ladies and Gentlemen, I know that I have only to mention the name of my grandmother, Nawab Sikandar Begam, to recall to your minds her courageous support of the British Government in the days of the mutiny. It was the same martial spirit which prompted my mother to equip and maintain a regiment of Imperial Service Cavalry. I, too, have my share of the fighting instinct, and since I became the ruler of the State one of my chief desires has been to promote the well-being and efficiency of the Bhopal Victoria

Lancers. It has always been my wish that my children should uphold the good traditions of their family; and it was on this account that I placed the Military Department under the charge of my second son, Colonel Obaidullah Khan. I have no hesitation in saying that, by the manner in which he has carried out the duties of his office, he has more than justified his appointment. It is a great satisfaction to me to know that his services have been appreciated by His Majesty the King-Emperor, by Your Excellency, and by His Excellency the Commander-in-Chief of the Indian Army.

Ladies and Gentlemen, I have trespassed too long upon your time, and I thank you most heartily for the patience with which you have listened to me. I have but one duty to perform before I sit down, and that is the extremely pleasant duty of asking you to drink to the health of Their Excellencies Lord and Lady Minto."

After the toast had been drunk, His Excellency rose and said :

'YOUR HIGHNESS, LADIES AND GENTLEMEN,

Your Highness has told me that this is the first occasion on which a Viceroy has visited your State during your rule. I can only assure Your Highness that it is all the greater pleasure to me to feel that I am the first representative of the King-Emperor to receive your splendid hospitality. To me the occasion is very full of meaning for, as Your Highness has reminded me in such eloquent words, it has fallen to my lot, as the great-grandson of a former Lord Minto, to revive the recollections of the friendly, *kharita* which 100 years ago laid the foundations of that friendship which has existed, through many trials and storms, between Bhopal and the British Government down to the present day. During all that time the Rulers of Bhopal have given many proofs of loyalty to the British Raj. Your Highness's grandmother, Your Highness's mother and you yourself have splendidly upheld the illustrious traditions of your State, and have given proof of devoted loyalty not only in words but in deeds. The troops of your ancestors and ancestresses have covered themselves with glory on many a hard-fought field, and when 20 years ago the Imperial Service Troops movement was initiated by Lord Dufferin, Your Highness's mother was one of the first amongst the great Indian Ruler to offer her support. The name Victoria Lancers linked them to the throne as the offering of a lady Ruler of an Indian State to the great Queen-Empress. And Your Highness, may I venture to say that the military spirit of your proud and martial house has descended in full measure upon yourself. You may well be proud of the efficiency to which Your Imperial Service Troops have now attained, and which the energy of their Commandant—Your Highness's son, Colonel Obaidullah Khan—has done so much to perfect. I am proud to have him as my Aide-de-Camp. I cannot help taking this opportunity of congratulating Your Highness on being the only lady Ruler of these modern peaceful days who has seen active service on the field. For a rumour has reached me that Your Highness, during your pilgrimage to Mecca, escorted by your own body-guard, had the good fortune to repel, with some loss to the enemy, an attack of Arab tribesmen who fell suddenly upon you. Possibly the attack was not entirely unwelcome to the warlike spirit of Your Highness's escort.

But it is not only to military organisation that you have devoted your attention. You have justly earned the reputation of a great administrator, and in the affairs of State the noble inspirations you have instilled into your sons have been rewarded by the able assistance of Nawab Nasrullah Khan. Your interest in the advance of education, especially in the higher education of Indian Chiefs, your recognition of the importance of religious instruction, your gifts to the Aligarh College and other institutions, your deep sympathy with the education of your own sex, your princely generosity towards the poor and destitute of your own faith, and your ideal that the landed aristocracy, by taking a leading part in the active life of the community should contribute to the stability of a Native State, have combined to set a valuable example of the duties of a great Chief, by the observance of which the stability of British rule in India will, I hope, for ever be justified and confirmed.

Your Highness, Lady Minto and I will always look back on our visit to you not only with many recollections of your hospitality, but with a sincere admiration for your devoted labours for the progress of your State and the welfare of your people. I thank you most cordially for the kind words with which you have proposed the toast of our healths.

And now, Ladies and Gentlemen, I will ask you to join with me in drinking to the happiness and prosperity of our distinguished hostess, Her Highness the Begam."

At the conclusion of His Excellency's speech the company moved on to the terrace to witness a display of fireworks. These had been specially manufactured for the occasion, some by an English, and others by an Indian firm. The star shells, and a set piece representing a fight between two battleships, were specially admired. On the termination of the display, *attar* and *pan* were distributed, and my guests departed.

At eight o'clock on the morning of November 12th, there was a review of the Imperial Service troops. His Excellency attended the review on horseback, and, accompanied by Colonel Obaidullah Khan, inspected the men and their horses, and watched their movements with the critical eye of an expert. After the troops had marched past, Colonel Obaidullah Khan and the officers came to the front, and His Excellency, in a short speech, expressed his satisfaction with all he had seen in the course of his inspection, and requested Colonel Obaidullah Khan to inform the men that he was greatly pleased with their discipline, and the soldierly qualities they had displayed. Colonel Obaidullah Khan translated this gracious message to his officers, who in turn communicated it to the men under their command. His Excellency then came to the tent where I was seated and complimented me on the efficiency of my troops. "You ought to be very proud of them," he said. "I am very pleased. The gallop past was splendid, and the whole of the cavalry and artillery are beautifully mounted."

At nine o'clock, we drove to the city, and His Excellency laid the foundation-stone of the Minto Hall. In requesting him to perform this ceremony I said :

"YOUR EXCELLENCY,

Last evening, in expressing the pleasure which it gave me to welcome Your Excellency to Bhopal, I spoke of the historical connection of your family with my State. It is because of that connection that I have so earnestly desired to have a permanent memorial of Your Excellency in my capital. By the opening of this building, which you have kindly permitted me to name the Minto Hall, that desire will now, to my great joy, be fulfilled. The need of a durbar, or reception hall in the vicinity of the Lal Koti and the Guest House has long been felt. In performing this ceremony, Your Excellency will be inaugurating a building which will be of great utility on public occasions, and will also add much to the comfort and convenience of honoured guests of the State."

Before laying the stone, His Excellency said :

"YOUR HIGHNESS,

I am very pleased to think that, by means of this Hall, my name and the name of my family will be preserved in Bhopal. This is but another example of that kindly courtesy for which Your Highness's name is proverbial throughout India. I hope that this Hall will not only fulfil the public objects for which it is so much needed, but that it will continue for all time to further Your Highness's generous hospitality, and the friendly relations of your British and Indian guests."

The ceremony was performed with the customary formalities ; and thus the official programme of His Excellency's visit was brought to a successful conclusion.

In the evening there was a garden-party at Ahmedabad. After tea the guests took part in shooting competitions and other games. I fired a shooting match with Lady Minto, which was watched with much interest. As all the arrangements for Their Excellencies' departure had already been made, they drove straight from Ahmedabad to the Railway Station, whither I accompanied them, and bade them good-bye on the platform. Their departure was private. My other guests remained at Bhopal till the following day, when I again entertained them at a garden-party. On this occasion, I fired a shooting match with Mrs. Daly.

The Countess of Minto

CHAPTER VI

SPORTS AND A MARRIAGE

WITH the approval of the Government of India, the Imperial Service Troops hold every year an athletic meeting at which competitions take place in all kinds of military games and exercises.

These meetings, the first of which was held six years ago, are productive of much good. They enable the officers and men selected to represent the different States to exchange views on military matters, and to compare the progress of their own regiments with that made by others, while the competitions engender a spirit of emulation which tends to promote the general efficiency of the service.

In the beginning of the year 1910, Colonel Obaidullah Khan told me that he would much like the meeting of that year to take place at Bhopal. I readily gave my consent, and invitations were issued to all the States maintaining Imperial Service regiments, the meeting being fixed for the latter half of February. My son, to whom the preparations were entrusted, entered upon his task with his wonted energy and enthusiasm. But a recent indisposition, the effects of which he was still feeling, prevented him from giving as much attention as he wished to the arrangements, and we were both extremely grateful for the timely assistance of Captain Pitcher, who very kindly came to Bhopal and took over the heavier portion of my son's duties.

The European officers who came to take part in the meeting were lodged in a camp pitched in the grounds of the Guest House, and two other camps were pitched for the Indian Officers and other ranks, one near the polo ground, and the other in the adjacent Hayat Afza garden. Officers and servants of the State were on duty day and night in each camp to look after the comforts and needs of the visitors. Cooked food was prepared for all who were Mussalmans, and rations were provided for Hindus. The following States, besides those of Central India, were represented at the meeting :—Kashmir, Patiala, Rampur, Bikanir, Bhawalpur, Khairpur, Jodhpur, Bharatpur, Faridkot, Jind, Malerkotla, Alwar, Kapurthala and Mysore.

The sports, which I went to see several times, commenced on the 23rd February. A polo tournament, the first ever held at these meetings, was the most important event on the programme. Besides the prizes given by me, a special cup to be competed for in this tournament was presented by General Drummond, and cups for each member of the winning team were presented by Colonel Obaidullah Khan.

On the last day of the meeting, I went to the polo ground and presented the prizes to the victors in the various competitions. I was gratified to learn that everything had passed off most successfully. The only untoward circumstance was the indisposition of Colonel Obaidullah Khan, and great regret was expressed on all sides that he had been unable to take an active part in the programme.

On the evening of the 26th, the European officers were entertained at a dinner at the Lal Kothi. I as usual, joined my guests at desert, and, when the royal toasts had been drunk, I proposed the health of General Drummond. My speech was as follows :—

"COLONEL DALY, GENERAL DRUMMOND, LADIES AND GENTLEMEN,

My first duty is to thank you all most heartily for the kindness you have done me by accepting my invitation to the Athletic Meeting which has just come to a close. I am delighted to have had this opportunity of welcoming you all to Bhopal; for what can be a greater pleasure than to meet old friends and to make the acquaintance of new ones? I sincerely hope that your stay here has been comfortable, and that the Indian officers and men who have responded to my invitation have thoroughly enjoyed their visit to Bhopal.

I congratulate all those who have competed in the sports on their excellent performances. By thus taking part in manly games and exercises, they are fostering that soldierly spirit which leads to the doing of brave deeds, and which will stand them in good stead should they be called upon to take the field under the flag of their King-Emperor.

As you are all aware, this is the first time in the history of these meetings that a polo tournament has figured in the programme. I regard this as a very welcome innovation. Polo is a game in which cavalry regiments take a special interest; and I hope that the Inspector-General of Imperial Service Troops and the Rulers of States will see their way to organising a similar tournament at every future meeting.

I desire to take this opportunity of thanking Colonel Grimston and Captain Pitcher for their great help in connection with the arrangements for these sports. My son, Colonel Obaidullah Khan, as you know, took charge of this work; but illness unfortunately prevented him from giving to it all the attention that it demanded. Thanks, however, to the timely assistance of the officers I have mentioned, everything continued to progress smoothly, and my son was relieved of all anxiety.

Ladies and Gentlemen, I now ask you to drink to the healths of Colonel and Mrs. Daly and General Drummond."

In replying to the toast General Drummond said:

"Your Highness,

Colonel Daly has allowed me to have the honour of thanking you most gratefully for the very kind words in which you have proposed his and Mrs. Daly's health and my own. In doing so, I desire also to thank you on behalf of all your guests for the splendid hospitality you have shown us during our stay in Bhopal, and to tell you how thoroughly we have enjoyed ourselves. And again, speaking in the name of the Imperial Service Troops, I desire to say how greatly all ranks appreciate Your Highness's kindness in inviting us to hold our seventh Athletic Meeting in your State, and how grateful we are for the admirable arrangements which have been made for the comfort and entertainment of the officers and men of the various corps who are assembled here. These arrangements have been perfect in every detail; and from start to finish the meeting has gone off without a hitch of any kind.

No less than 721 officers and men, from States as far apart as Jammu and Mysore, have come to Bhopal to take part in these sports, and every event on the programme has been contested with keenness, and in a thoroughly sporting and manly spirit. Every year the breaking of records becomes a harder task. But I am pleased to say that this year a new record in these sports for the half-mile has been created, and the previous record for the high-jump has been equalled. The polo tournament, to which Your Highness has alluded, may be regarded as a record for the Bhopal State, since this is the first time that such a tournament has been held at one of our meetings. All the games were keenly contested, and the final result was a victory for the Bhopal Victoria Lancers. While we all acknowledge the good play of the other teams, we cannot but be pleased at the well-earned success of Your Highness's own fine horsemen.

In the preparations for this meeting, most valuable help was given by Your Highness's officers. Where all worked so hard and willingly, it seems invidious on my part to mention any names. I feel sure, however, Your Highness will be glad to know that the following officers have been specially energetic and useful: Major Karim Beg, Major Qaiyum Khan, Commandant Iqbal Muhammad, Mr. Amir Ahmad, Mr. Safdar Ali Khan, and Risaldar Mumtaz Husain Khan. I have also to offer my special thanks to Nawab Nasrullah Khan and Nawab Obaidullah Khan for the great interest they have taken in the meeting. Though suffering from a trying indisposition, Colonel Obaidullah Khan has pluckily worked day and night to make the arrangements as complete and perfect as possible. We all hope for his speedy restoration to health. Finally, our warmest thanks are due to Your Highness for the personal interest which you have taken in this gathering, and which has contributed more than anything else to its success. Your guests will carry away with them the liveliest recollections of their happy stay in your State, and will never forget your great kindness to them. We all hope that Your Highness will long be spared to continue your wise rule, and that your great State will ever flourish and prosper.

Ladies and Gentlemen, I ask you to fill your glasses, and join me in drinking to the health of Her Highness the Begam of Bhopal."

On the afternoon of the next day I gave a garden-party at Ahmedabad, and the same evening all my visitors departed.

A few days later Bhopal was again *en fête*, the occasion being the betrothal ceremony of Sahibzada Muhammad Habibullah Khan and Sahibzadi Birjis Jahan Begam, between whom a marriage had recently been arranged by Nawab Nasrullah Khan and Colonel Obaidullah Khan. The ceremony took place on the 14th March. Among the guests I invited to Bhopal to witness it, were the Hon'ble Colonel Daly and Mrs. Daly, the Political Agent and Mrs. Bayley, and other European friends, all of whom reached Bhopal on the evening of the 13th.

At nine o'clock on the morning of the 14th, I paid a formal visit to my guests, and, in the afternoon, I was at home to them at the Rahat Manzil. All the officers of the State were entertained by Nawab Nasrullah Khan at the Sadar Manzil, where at 5 o'clock, a procession was formed to conduct Habibullah Khan to the Rahat Manzil. The *Mahi Maratib*, preceded by a band, headed the procession. Detachments of infantry and mounted troops came next, followed by a host of attendants bearing on their heads trays of fruits and sweet-meats, and behind these came the State coach in which the bridegroom was seated accompanied by his uncle, Sahibzada Hamidullah Khan, his brother Sahibzada Rafiqullah Khan, and Munshi Israr Hasan Khan, the Judicial Minister. The coach was escorted by a body of Imperial Service cavalry, and was followed by carriages containing the Sardars and officers of the State.

As the procession approached the entrance to the Rahat Manzil, the younger brothers of the bridegroom, Sahibzadas Wahid-uz-zafar Khan and Syad-uz-zafar Khan, following an ancient Bhopal custom, closed the gates, and refused to open them until toll had been paid. The procession came to a standstill, and it was only after Nawab Nasrullah Khan had paid the traditional sum of five hundred rupees, that it was allowed to pass in.

When the State coach reached the portico of the palace, it was received with showers of gold *mohurs* and rupees. Habibullah Khan ascended to the terrace on which my guests and the members of my family had assembled to watch his arrival, while the Khans and officers who arrived with him took the seats provided for them in the verandah below. In the guest-chamber, the Hon'ble Colonel Daly, Major Bayley, Nawab Nasrullah Khan, Sahibzada Hamidullah Khan, and six of the chief nobles of the State, were seated each with a *pandan* in front of him. These they filled with money as the bridegroom appeared; but only the money in the *pandans* of the Nawab Sahib and Hamidullah Khan was accepted. Colonel Obaidullah Khan presented Habibullah Khan with a splendid *khilat*, and the Nawab Sahib gave a corresponding present to Birjis Jahan Begam, together with many costly jewels. I conferred on Habibullah Khan the title, Sikandar Jah Birjis Dulha, and on Birjis Jahan Begam the title, Shamsa Taj Habib Dulhan. On the conclusion of the ceremonies, a move was made to the gardens, where I entertained my guests with various amusements till sunset.

On the morning of the 15th, the Agent to the Governor-General, attended by the Nasir-ul-muham, visited the Jail, the Prince of Wales Hospital, the Sulaimania School, and the Alexandra High School. There was a gymkhana in the afternoon, and a dinner at the Lal Kothi in the evening. I joined my guests at the end of the dinner, and, after the toast of the King-Emperor, I proposed the health of Colonel Daly in the following terms:

"COLONEL DALY, LADIES AND GENTLEMEN,

It is a very great pleasure to me to welcome you to Bhopal, and to see myself surrounded, at this time, by so many old friends. Before I touch on any other matters, I wish to take this opportunity of thanking His Majesty's Government for conferring on my son, Colonel Obaidullah Khan, the honorary rank of Captain in the British army. During the time that he has been in charge of the Military

Department, Colonel Obaidullah Khan has, indeed, done most valuable work for the State, and I am extremely grateful to Colonel Daly, Major Bayley, and the Inspecting Officers of the Imperial Service Troops for recognising and bringing his services to notice.

Ladies and Gentlemen, I have on several previous occasions referred to the various administrative measures and changes that have marked the 9th year of my rule, and also to the valuable assistance I have received throughout the year from my Revenue and Judicial Ministers. I do not, therefore, propose to speak of these matters in detail this evening. I should like, however, to say one or two words about the revenue administration, and to mention the excellent work that has been done by Syad Nasir-ud-din in connection with the introduction of the 19 years' settlement, which is shortly to replace the unsatisfactory five years system that has hitherto been followed. Thanks to the energy of Syad Nasir-ud-din, the new scheme is rapidly approaching completion, and I have every hope that it will be possible to commence the distribution of leases in April next, and that by the month of June the 19 years' settlement will be in operation. I have always held that such systems should be framed in the best interests, not only of the State, but of the cultivators; and in drafting the terms of the new settlement, I have kept this principle steadily in view. I am exceedingly obliged to Mr. Hoare for giving me the benefit of his wide experience in revenue matters, and to Colonel Daly for sparing this officer to come to Bhopal to assist me with his advice. The work of dealing with arrears of revenue has also, I am glad to say, made good progress, and by the time the new settlement comes into force, we shall, I hope, be able to show a clean slate. In two of the three districts of the State this work is being carried out under my personal directions, and in the third district under the directions of the Revenue Minister, who is devoting himself to this difficult duty with his customary zeal and ability. In connection with all these matters, it gives me great pleasure to say that I have received most able assistance from Nawab Nasrullah Khan, who has discharged to my complete satisfaction the various important duties that have been entrusted to him.

And now, Ladies and Gentlemen, having done with business affairs may I turn for a moment to the event which has brought us together, an event which, I am sure, has interested not only Colonel Daly, who is, as it were, an hereditary friend of my family, but all the other kind friends whom I see around me this evening. We have just celebrated the betrothal of my grandson Sahibzada Habibullah Khan, the son of Nawab Nasrullah Khan, to my grand-daughter Sahibzadi Birjis Jahan Begam, the daughter of Colonel Obaidullah Khan. This alliance will give additional strength to those feelings of brotherly affection which have always existed between my two elder sons; I trust that there may be many such alliances in my family, and that they may ever serve to draw its members into closer and closer unity. Colonel Daly, may I say that it is with no ordinary feelings of pleasure that I welcome you to Bhopal on this happy occasion. Nearly forty years ago, your distinguished father was a guest at my own marriage; and you yourself were a guest at the marriage of my son Sahibzada Hamidullah Khan. I, therefore, look upon it as a most auspicious and happy circumstance that you have been present at the marriage of my grandchildren. On this occasion, too, I have the additional and very great pleasure of welcoming Mrs. Daly, who I know is interested in all that concerns my family, and who, as a member of my own sex, will understand all that this marriage means to me, and how eagerly I have looked forward to its celebration.

Ladies and Gentlemen, I thank you very heartily for coming here to take part in these rejoicings, and I hope your visit has been a very pleasant one. In conclusion I pray for the health and happiness of His Majesty the King-Emperor, and that he may long be spared to rule over his faithful subjects."

Before sitting down I asked my guests to drink to the health of Colonel and Mrs. Daly. When the toast had been drunk, Colonel Daly rose and returned thanks on behalf of Mrs. Daly and himself. In the course of his speech he congratulated Colonel Obaidullah Khan on being made a Captain in the British army, and warmly commended the work he had done for the State army and the Imperial Service Lancers. The latter he said had been brought to a very high state of efficiency, and were now a regiment of which any Ruler might well be proud. He then complimented me on the reforms which I was introducing into the revenue administration and said that he had no doubt that the new settlement would prove of the greatest advantage both to my subjects and to the State. Mr. Hoare, he added, would be very pleased to know that he had been of assistance to me, and I could rest assured that he would always count it a pleasure to render me or my Durbar any service within his power. He also referred to other features of my administration, and was kind enough to conclude his remarks on this subject by saying "I never come to Bhopal but I see on every side some new sign of Your Highness's solicitude for the well-being and happiness of your subjects." After alluding to the long and friendly connection of his family with Bhopal, he said that it gave him and Mrs. Daly the greatest pleasure, a pleasure which he was sure was shared by all my guests, to be present on such an important occasion as the marriage of my grandchildren. He wished the bride and bridegroom every happiness in their future lives, and brought his speech to an end by thanking me for my hospitality, and proposing my health.

In the following July, on the 21st day of the month, a daughter was born in the palace of Nawab Nasrullah Khan. I was at the palace when this happy event took place. I had naturally looked forward with joy to the arrival of a new grandchild, and when the little stranger proved to be a new grand-daughter my happiness was complete; for I felt that this girl whom God had sent to me would grow up to help me in my efforts to better the lives of the women of India, which I regarded as my special mission in life. The *aqiqah* ceremony, which had been described in the first volume of my *Memoirs*, took place on the seventh day, and at my suggestion the child received the name Nur Jahan Begam.

To complete the administrative machinery of the new settlement, I this year established a Land Records Office, for the preservation of all documents relating to the tenure of land. All changes made were to be carefully recorded, so that a complete history of the revenue administration of every village might be available at a moment's notice. A survey class for the training of village *patwaris* was opened, and this, as well as the model farms, which I established at the same time, were placed under the management of the Land Records Office. The farms were to be run on the most approved scientific lines, that they might serve as models for *mustajirs* and cultivators, and so lead, in time, to the general improvement of the agriculture of the State. Three villages were set apart for this purpose, and an adequate sum was sanctioned for the organization of the farms.

Another of my experiments was the establishment of a sugar factory on the lines recommended by the Assistant Director of Agriculture in the United Provinces. I did this in the hope that, if the experiment proved successful and profitable, other factories would be started by private individuals, and a new impetus would thus be given to the cultivation of the sugar-cane. The factory was located at Ichhawar, as the cane was extensively grown in the Ichhawar *tahsil*.

It is, as a rule, impossible for a cultivator to improve his holding unless he receives help from the State. Grants for this purpose, known as *taqavi*, had from time to time been made ; but the practice had been discontinued because the money thus advanced was never repaid, and was seldom used for the purposes for which it was intended. I have always held that advances are necessary ; and that, under business-like management and careful supervision, the *taqavi* system is beneficial both for the cultivators and for the State. As soon, therefore, as the arrangements for the new settlements were completed, I re-introduced the system, and issued at the same time a set of regulations to ensure the proper application of all money advanced, and the repayment of the same in due course.

This year, the local rates due from the villages of *jagirdars* were for the first time collected according to a fixed and uniform scale. There had always been great difficulty in realizing these dues, and many *jagirdars* were heavily in debt to the State. It was now decided that arrears due from *jagirdars* who came under the jurisdiction of the courts, should be recovered by the same process used in dealing with ordinary defaulters.

Of the various other administrative acts and events of this year, it must suffice to mention the following:

(1) Up to this time, the financial year had been computed on the lunar system. As the drawbacks to this system had long been apparent, it was decided to abolish it, and the *fasli* calendar was adopted for revenue purposes.

(2) The boundaries of the Gwalior State were marked by cactus hedges. It was found that in certain places, where Bhopal territory marched with that of Gwalior, the cactus hedge had been planted on the Bhopal side of the boundary. The matter was taken up with the Gwalior Durbar, and a satisfactory settlement was arrived at.

(3) Under the then existing system, the proce-

dure in the Law Courts provided for no less than five appeals. This not only prevented the quick disposal of cases, but put litigants to much expense and trouble. To remove these disadvantages, the procedure was modified so as to admit of only three appeals. Further, to lessen the heavy and constantly increasing work of the Judicial Minister, full judiciary powers were given to the Assistant Judicial Minister, who was created a Puisne Judge. This has made it possible for the Judicial Minister, when he deems it expedient, to transfer appeals from his own to the Assistant's court.

(4) The State sent a number of experienced and intelligent *mustajirs* to the Agricultural Exhibition held this year at Lahore, in order that they might see the results of recent agricultural experiments, and become acquainted with the most modern farm implements and machinery, and the right methods of using them.

(5) One day, the students of the Sultania school were brought to see me. I talked to them a long time about their studies, and incidentally learnt a good deal about the state of primary education in Bhopal. I was glad to find that the attendance in the Urdu schools was steadily increasing, for this showed that even amongst the poorer classes of the Muhammadan community the benefits of education were beginning to be realized; but I was disappointed that so few children were being taught the English language. I was told that this was due partly to the in-

difference of parents and guardians, but that in many cases the poorer classes could not afford to send their children to schools where English was taught. I, therefore, issued instructions that poor children and orphans were to receive State scholarships of 3 and 5 rupees a month to enable them to attend higher grade schools. In the case of those whose parents could afford the necessary fees, attendance was made compulsory.

(6) I opened this year a fancy bazar for the exhibition and sale of embroidery and needlework executed by purdah women in Bhopal. I hoped by this means to induce people to send their daughters to the institutions where instruction in fancy work and other feminine arts is provided. A small fee was charged for entrance to the bazar, and two days in each week were reserved for men. The attendance was very satisfactory, and much interest was taken in the exhibits, many of which fetched a good price.

(7) At the beginning of this year, the Ahmedabad palace was the only building in Bhopal that was lit by electricity. Steps were now taken for supplying electric light to the whole city, a project which I had long had in mind The power station was erected below the Moti Mahal, on the edge of the lake. Before the end of the year the city palaces and the main road from the Lal Kothi to Ahmedabad were illuminated. The supply was gradually extended to shops and private houses, the owners being charged only

the actual cost of production for the light they used.

(8) During the hot weather, I went for a change of air to Pachmarhi, and remained there two weeks. Though less cold and less fashionable than Simla or Naini Tal, Pachmarhi is a very beautiful place, with a pleasant and bracing climate. During the summer months it is the head-quarters of the Government of the Central Provinces, and many officers are sent there each year for training in musketry. In the course of my short visit I had the pleasure of meeting the Hon'ble Mr. Phillips, the Chief Commissioner of the Central Provinces, and Mrs. Phillips, and also Mr. Laurie, the Commissioner of the Narbada district, and Mrs. Laurie. All the officials of the Government were most kind in making arrangements for my comfort and convenience; and I deeply appreciated the warm welcome extended to me by the residents of the station.

CHAPTER VII

THE DEATH OF KING EDWARD VII

SHORTLY after noon on the 7th May, 1910, I received the following telegram from the Political Agent at Sehore:

"Reuter reports that His Majesty King Edward is dead."

This distressing and unlooked-for news was a great shock to me, and caused widespread sorrow throughout Bhopal. I immediately ordered the flags on the palaces and the fort to be lowered to half-mast, and issued a notification that all public offices and bazars were to be closed for the space of three days. At the same time I sent the following telegram to the Political Agent:

"Am deeply grieved to hear of His Majesty's death. Shall be exceedingly obliged if you will cable my heart-felt and sincerest condolences to His Royal Highness the Prince of Wales, Her Majesty the Queen and Royal Family"

In reply to my message, I received the following cable from His Majesty King George V:

"Accept my sincere thanks for your kind message of sympathy."

GEORGE, R. & I.

The official announcement of the death of the King-Emperor, which was received by cable from the Secretary of State, was published in Notifica-

H. I. M. King Edward VII.

tion 1105 of the Home Department on May 9th. The funeral ceremony took place on May 20th. I was then at Mussoorie, where I received a telegram from the Political Agent in regard to the manner in which the day was to be observed; and this I sent on to the Muin-ul-muham for his guidance. A day of public mourning was proclaimed throughout the State. All business was suspended, and all public offices and schools were closed. In the evening, sixty-eight minute guns were fired from the fort, the number corresponding with his late Majesty's age. The last gun was fired as the sun set.

King Edward's death was mourned throughout the world, for he was the friend not only of his own subjects, but of all mankind. He laboured for the peace of the world, and posterity has justly named him the Peace-maker. As Prince of Wales he won the hearts of all with whom he came in contact by the charm of his manner, and the frankness of his speech. The pledges which he gave at his accession to safeguard the interests, and respect the rights of his people were amply redeemed in the years that followed. Honour and justice characterized all his dealings, and throughout his reign his love of peace and justice, his high sense of honour, and the many other virtues he inherited from his noble mother, gained for him, as they gained for her, the respect and admiration of all nations.

There is no country where King Edward's name

will be remembered with stronger feelings of gratitude than in India. His message of good-will, read at the memorable durbar held in honour of his coronation, filled the hearts of his Indian subjects with joy and hope, and from that day his solicitation for their welfare never abated. In times of distress his sympathy was always forth-coming. A single example will suffice to show how deep and sincere that sympathy was. In August, 1907, when plague was raging in many parts of India, the Viceroy received from His Majesty the following letter :

"MY DEAR VICEROY,

I have followed with anxious interest the later course of that epidemic of plague by which India has for eleven years past been so sorely afflicted.

The welfare of my Indian subjects must ever be to me an object of high concern, and I am deeply moved when I think of the misery that has been borne with such silent patience in all those stricken homes.

I am well aware how unremitting have been the efforts of Your Excellency's predecessors and yourself to make out the causes of the pestilence, and to mitigate its effects.

It is my earnest hope and prayer that the further measures now being prepared by Your Excellency, in consultation with zealous and able officers, may be crowned with merciful success.

I desire you to communicate this expression of my heartfelt sympathy to my Indian subjects.

Believe me,
My dear Viceroy,
Sincerely yours,
EDWARD, R. & I.

In the year 1909, King Edward gave his royal assent to the Indian Reforms Bill. Of all that he did for India, there was nothing which called forth deeper feelings of gratitude. By the provisions of this Bill, the people of India were given for the first time a definite share in the government of their country. They had the further gratification of seeing an Indian gentleman, in the person of Mr. Sinha, appointed to the Executive Council of the Governor-General, while the Right Hon'ble Syad Amir Ali was given a seat on the Judicial Committee of the Privy Council.

The loyalty of Bhopal to the British throne dates from the foundation of the State. History records many instances of services rendered to the paramount Power by the Rulers of the State, and of the generous manner in which such services were acknowledged and requited. The mutual regard and confidence thus created have increased with the passage of years, and were never more firmly established than they are to-day. In the year 1875, while on a visit to Calcutta with my mother, I had the honour of being presented to His Majesty, then Prince of Wales. In the course of this interview, which is fully described in the first volume of my Memoirs, His Majesty said to me, " At this time, you and I are in similar positions. You are the Crown Princess of Bhopal, and I am the Crown Prince of England." It was a curious coincidence that His Majesty ascended the throne of the British Empire on the same day that I became Ruler of Bhopal.

In the course of his reign, His Majesty honoured me with many marks of his regard. Amongst these there was none that I prized more highly than the letter in his own handwriting which he was graciously pleased to send me at the time of his coronation in acknowledgment of my congratulatory address. In the year 1904, I had the honour of being made a Grand Commander of the Indian Empire, and in the year 1910, I was made a Grand Commander of the Star of India.

It had been my intention, on the completion of the various administrative schemes I had in hand, to present myself at the Imperial court, and personally express my devotion to His Majesty, and my gratitude for the favours I had received at his royal hands. But God willed otherwise: and before I could offer my thanks to my benefactor, I was mourning his loss.

In India, as in all parts of the world, the tidings of King Edward's death caused deep and widespread grief. In every household signs of mourning were visible, and afforded striking testimony to the loyalty of the people, and of their affection for the person of their late Ruler. In India, too, the utmost sympathy was felt for Queen Alexandra in her bereavement. I think only those of her own sex, who have passed through a like trial, can realize how heavy her sorrow was. Queen Alexandra shared not only the throne of her august husband, but his power to win the love of his subjects. She was admired, and beloved both as a queen and as a woman. Her manifold graces, and the charm of her manners and conversation delighted all who attended her court, while her bounty, her sympathy for the sick and suffering, and her interest in all that concerned the lives of those around her, endeared her alike to rich and poor, to high and low. Her immense popularity was shown by the thousands of messages of sympathy which at this sad time, poured in upon her from every quarter of the globe. The letter in which these messages were publicly acknowledged, revealed the bitterness of her affliction ; but it told also of her reliance on God, and patient submission to His will. I have read this letter through many times, and it has always strengthened and comforted me.

The official announcement of the accession to the throne of His Majesty King George V was received on the 8th of May. At five o'clock on the evening of that day, flags were raised to full mast, and a royal salute of 101 guns was fired. On the following morning flags were again lowered to half mast, and remained so until the end of the period of mourning. Copies of the Royal Proclamation announcing the accession, of the official notifications relating to the coronation, and of His Majesty's gracious message to the Princes and peoples of India, were sent to me, and were published in the State gazette. His Majesty's words were read throughout the country with feelings of joy and hope.

Speaking at a banquet which took place at the Guildhall to welcome him on his return from his Indian tour, King George, then the Prince of Wales, said, "A large element of sympathy is required in the administration of India." These words, uttered in an assemblage of great statesmen and leaders of public opinion, created a deep and lasting impression on the minds of the Indian people. They were recalled when he ascended the throne, and the thought of being ruled by one who had thus proclaimed himself the friend of India, filled every heart with thankfulness. I am confident that the son and successor of King Edward, the Peace-maker, will never lack the loyal homage and obedience of the king-loving people of this land, and that under his benign protection the prosperity and progress of his eastern dominions will become greater day by day.

H. I. M. King George V.

CHAPTER VIII

ILLNESS OF COLONEL OBAIDULLAH KHAN

For some time before Lord Minto's visit to Bhopal, my son Colonel Obaidullah Khan had been suffering from enlargement of the liver. He had been treated by Dr. Grasswood, and for a time his health seemed to improve. But the heavy work which engaged him night and day during His Excellency's visit was a severe strain on him, and he again became very unwell, though outwardly he appeared to be in good health. As it had already been arranged that he should join His Excellency's staff at Calcutta, and take part in the New Year's day celebrations, he left Bhopal towards the end of December, and was for some days a guest at Government House, where he was most hospitably entertained, both His Excellency and Lady Minto showing him much kindness. On the 30th December, he and Sir Partab Singh were in attendance on His Excellency at a military review. After the review he was again indisposed; but he made light of the matter, and on the following day took part in a polo match. In the evening the unfavourable symptoms returned; he suffered much uneasiness, and passed a sleepless night.

On New Year's day, the *Gazette of India* contained the announcement that I had been created a G.C.S.I. On learning this, Colonel Obaidullah Khan, desiring to congratulate me personally on my new honour, begged permission to return to Bhopal. His Excellency graciously granted his request, at the same time expressing his regret at the early termination of his visit.

My son left Calcutta for Bhopal on the 2nd January. He was unwell at the time of his departure, and on reaching Benares he felt so ill that he decided to break his journey, and take the advice of the Civil Surgeon. But the doctor's medicines gave him no relief and after a short rest, he resumed his journey. At Lucknow he again halted and consulted Dr. Chedar, with no better results. When he eventually reached Bhopal his condition had become worse. He arrived at midnight, and at four o'clock in the morning a motor car was sent to fetch me from Ahmedabad to the Humayun Manzil. I was much upset and agitated; but was relieved when I reached the palace to find the patient somewhat recovered. I immediately telegraphed for Colonel Roberts, the Residency Surgeon at Indore, and for Major Haig, the Agency Surgeon. Mrs. Barnes was also summoned, and before noon all three doctors had arrived. A consultation took place, and it was unanimously agreed that my son was suffering from neurasthenia. Treatment for this complaint was accordingly prescribed and commenced; but in spite of it, the patient's health grew daily worse, and it was decided that he should seek change of air, and fresh medical advice in Bombay. He was accompanied thither by Munshi Israr Hasan Khan, and was placed under the treatment of Colonel Meyer, who, after examining him, strongly recommended a sea-voyage. Passages were, therefore, taken in the P. & O. steamship *Salsette* and my son, still accompanied by Munshi Israr Hasan Khan, set out for Aden. He was looked after during the voyage by the ship's doctor, but derived no benefit from his treatment. He had no sleep throughout the voyage, and suffered much from sea-sickness. The doctor who was consulted at Aden, a brother of the medical officer of the *Salsette*, also diagnosed his complaint as neurasthenia.

As no improvement had resulted from the voyage to Aden, it was decided not to proceed further, but to return, after a few days' rest, to Bhopal. On reaching Bombay, my son again saw Dr. Meyer. Dr. Chaila and Dr. Rao were also called in, and another consultation took place. This time the case was pronounced to be one of heart-strain due to over-work.

Colonel Roberts, who saw my son on his return to Bhopal, strongly advised him to leave the Humayun Manzil, and take up his residence outside the city, where he would enjoy purer air and pleasanter surroundings. I arranged, therefore, that he should come to Ahmedabad, where he would have the advantage of a more salubrious climate, and be at the same time under my personal care. Colonel Roberts, who was unremitting in his attentions, remained four days in Bhopal in order that he might watch the patient at night when the symptoms generally became more pronounced.

At this time, I chanced to see in the papers an advertisement of a Sanatorium which had recently been opened at Mussoorie, where persons suffering from heart trouble underwent a course of baths, which was said to be very efficacious. I consulted Colonel Roberts on the subject, and, with his approval, arranged to take my son to Mussoorie to make trial of this treatment. My Private Secretary, Munshi Sakhawat Husain, was sent in advance to secure accommodation for us, and I also wrote to Captain Ellwood, whom I have mentioned in a previous volume of my *Memoirs*, and who was at this time Commandant of the Mussoorie and Dehra Dun Volunteers, and he very kindly gave Sakhawat Husain his assistance. The house selected for us was one belonging to the Maharani of Jind, situated on Horn Hill. The rent was Rs. 3,000 a month, but, as we were in a hurry to go, I decided to take it.

We set out from Bhopal in the middle of May. The Shahriar Dulhan Sahiba, who had been suffering from jaundice and fever, and was also in need of a change of air, accompanied us. On reaching Rajpur, we received a message from Captain Ellwood to say that, as it was very cold in Mussoorie, it would not be advisable for us to arrive there at night-time; and, as both Colonel Obaidullah Khan and the Dulhan Sahiba were much fatigued by their long journey, we decided to spend the night in the Prince of Wales Hotel at Rajpur.

I had ordered a *jhapan* to be in readiness at Dehra Dun to take my son up the hill, as I feared that riding might be bad for his complaint. But he bravely decided to make the ascent on horseback. He was very tired when we reached our destination, but his spirits rose under the influence of the bracing air, and the beauty and novelty of the scenery. No time was lost in taking medical advice. Colonel Rainy and Dr. Mankle, two of the leading doctors of Mussoorie, were consulted. Their opinion of the case was identical with that given by the doctors of Bombay. The patient, they said, was suffering from general exhaustion brought on by over-work, while the heart had been weakened by repeated attacks of malaria.

The sanatorium where the consultation took place was distant only three miles from our residence; but even after this short journey my son was completely worn out. During the night which followed he was unable to obtain a moment's sleep, and suffered more pain and uneasiness than he had hitherto experienced. Mrs. Barnes, whom I had brought with me, attended him, and in the morning, Dr. Mankle was called in. He again made a careful examination of the heart, stomach, and liver, and strongly urged a course of electric baths. As I felt confidence in Dr. Mankle, I placed the case entirely in his hands, and my son, to avoid the fatigue of going backwards and forwards, took up his residence at the sanatorium. In addition to electric baths, his body was rubbed all over every day with olive oil. This treatment did him much good, and in a short time he was able to ride ten or fifteen miles daily without fatigue.

Whilst at Mussoorie, I made the acquaintance of several European ladies. Amongst them was Mrs. Brown, the wife of the Commissioner, with whom I enjoyed many friendly meetings. Both Mr. and Mrs. Brown visited me at Jind House, and I returned their calls.

Shortly after my arrival at Mussoorie, I attended a sad and solemn ceremony. This was the memorial service held on the occasion of the burial of His late Majesty, King Edward VII, which took place on May 14th. I took with me Mrs. Barnes and Munshi Israr Hasan Khan. Colonel Obaidullah Khan was too unwell to go. The service, which took place at 4-30 in the afternoon, was attended by all the troops in the station, and the students of the Mussoorie schools. A sermon was preached by the clergyman, after which hymns suited to the occasion were sung by the school children. All present wore mourning and signs of sorrow were visible on every face. It was an impressive ceremony, and it brought forcibly to my mind the transitoriness and instability of all earthly things. As I recalled the virtues and noble deeds of the departed monarch, I seemed to see before me his well-known features and majestic figure.

After the termination of the period of public mourning, Mrs. Brown gave a ladies' party in my honour, and I also gave a party, in the name of Birjis Jahan Begam, to the European children in Mussoorie. Mrs. Ellwood kindly undertook the arrangements of this entertainment, to which parents as well as children were invited. The house was decorated by Mr. Amir Ahmad, and refreshments were supplied by a well-known local catering firm. Mr. Brown, the Commissioner, was amongst the guests. Mrs. Brown, whom I had hoped to see, was unable to come owing to a previous engagement. At the end of the party I presented toys and other gifts to the children.

Meanwhile the Colonel Sahib, though not fully recovered, had derived considerable benefit from the treatment he had undergone; and, as the climate was now growing colder each day, and as some cases of cholera had occurred in the neighbourhood, it was decided to bring our sojourn on the hills to an end. I was anxious for other reasons not to prolong my absence from Bhopal. I had already been away for two months, and there were numerous State affairs which needed my personal attention. I had also to make arrangements for my forthcoming visit to Simla; and, in addition, I had just received news that the Hon'ble Colonel Daly was about to be transferred to Hyderabad, and I could not bear the idea of his leaving Central India without my having had an opportunity of bidding him good-bye, and thanking him for the many kindnesses I had met with at his hands.

Colonel Obaidullah Khan's health was so much improved that he rode on horseback from Mussoorie to Rajpur without experiencing any fatigue whatever. When we reached Dehra Dun, Dr. Walter took a skiogram of his heart. In the course of our journey to Bhopal, we halted at Piran Kaliar Sharif, to offer prayers at the shrine of the great saint Hazrat Dabir Sahib, and also at Aligarh, where Sahibzada Hamidullah Khan had just been installed as a student of the M. A. O. College. Here, as on our way to Mussoorie, Colonel Obaidullah Khan was examined by Hakim Muhammad Ajmal Khan. The Hakim Sahib spoke reassuringly about my son's health, and gave him some medicines. He told me that he had himself suffered from my son's complaint, but that his health was now greatly improved, though the disease was not entirely cured.

I was anxious that the Colonel Sahib should again see Dr. Meyer. So, after a few days' rest at Bhopal, I took him to Bombay. Dr. Meyer expressed his satisfaction at the progress he had made, and his encouraging report greatly comforted me.

I must not forget to mention that my son was, for a time, under the treatment of Hakim Syad Nur-ul-hasan, the chief Yunani doctor in Bhopal. The Hakim was unremitting in his attention to the patient, and his tonics often proved efficacious. Both at Ahmedabad and at Mussoorie, Mrs. Barnes proved herself a devoted and skilful nurse. Her help was invaluable, and her presence during these trying days was an immense comfort to me.

I give thanks to the Great Healer that my son is now convalescent. I trust that, by the grace of the same Beneficent Power, I shall soon see him restored to perfect health.

CHAPTER IX

A FAREWELL BANQUET

I HAVE said above that I visited Aligarh on my way back from Mussoorie in order to see my youngest son, Sahibzada Hamidullah Khan, who had just joined the Aligarh College. I will now explain why I sent the Sahibzada to that institution instead of to one of the Chiefs' Colleges. I have always been strongly in favour of Chiefs' Colleges. I hold that in India to-day it is not only important but essential that separate institutions should exist for the training of the sons of Chiefs and other persons of position. I cannot, however, regard the courses of study at present followed in these Colleges as satisfactory. In my opinion the standard aimed at is not sufficiently high. The students get an excellent general training, but they do not acquire the educational qualifications afforded by a university career. This seems to me a grave disadvantage, and I have long advocated the establishment of a Chiefs' university. I have written several pamphlets on this subject which I have submitted to the Council of the Daly College at Indore, and my suggestions are still under consideration.

It had always been my desire that Sahibzada Hamidullah Khan should take a university degree and it was with this end in view that I sent him to the Alexandra High School at Bhopal, which is affiliated to the university of Allahabad. I also hoped that by so doing I should induce other parents to send their sons to the school. In this I was not disappointed. The Sahibzada's attendance led to a marked increase in the number of students; while his good manners, and diligent attention to his studies had an excellent effect on the behaviour and work of his school-fellows.

Long before he passed the matriculation examination, I began to consider what college I should send him to for the completion of his university course. I made enquiries about many different colleges, and constantly discussed the matter with my friends and advisers. Many suggested that the Sahibzada should be sent to a European university. I knew that there was no better educational training than that which is obtained at an English university; but I could not reconcile myself to the idea of sending my son, who was still in his boyhood, so far away; and I decided, to make the best selection I could from the colleges of India. I finally came to the conclusion that, for the training of a Muhammadan boy, there was no better institution in India than the Muhammadan Anglo-Oriental College at Aligarh, because here the student receives instruction not only in secular subjects, but in the religion of his fathers. He is taught at the same time to be loyal to the British throne, while he learns to understand the ideals and aspirations of the Muhammadan community in India.

Having come to this decision, I wrote to Nawab Viqar-ul-mulk, the Honorary Secretary of the College, telling him that I proposed to send the Sahibzada to Aligarh without delay, to complete there his preparation for the ensuing matriculation examination. A house large enough to accommodate both the Sahibzada and Mr. Payne, who was to accompany him in the capacity of tutor and guardian, was secured near the College. It had formerly been the residence of the late Maulavi Saminullah Khan. All the arrangements were completed by the beginning of June, and the Sahibzada proceeded to Aligarh whilst I was still at Mussoorie. As Mr. Payne was then on leave in England, he stayed for a time with Mr. J. H. Towle, the Principal of the College.

Being anxious to see for myself what arrangements had been made for my son's education, and as I had often wished to see the College of which I had heard so much, I wrote from Mussoorie to Nawab Mushtaq Husain to say that I proposed to spend a short time at Aligarh on my way back to Bhopal. I told him that I wished my visit to be a purely informal one, and begged that no special arrangements should be made for my reception, but that I should be regarded as just an ordinary visitor who was interested in the welfare of the College. I received a reply from the Nawab Sahib assuring me that my wishes should be scrupulously regarded.

I took with me to Aligarh only Colonel Obaidullah Khan, Munshi Israr Hasan Khan, the Nasir-ul-muham, and a small personal staff. As my visit was of a private character all the arrangements for my stay were made by Sahibzada Hamidullah Khan, though he received every assistance from the College authorities. I was received at the railway station by Nawab Nizammilullah Khan, joint Honorary Secretary of the College, who accompanied me to Pahasu House, where I took up my quarters with Colonel Obaidullah Khan and the Shahriar Dulhan. The Nasir-ul-muham and the other members of my party occupied the house of Maulavi Saminullah Khan, which is close to Pahasu House. The next morning at 7 a.m. I paid an informal visit to the College. Nawab Nizammillullah Khan and the Colonel Sahib came with me, and we were escorted by the College riding squadron. I was greatly struck by the discipline and military bearing of these lads.

The Trustees, the Principal, and the Secretary-in-charge received us at the main entrance to the College. The Principal then conducted us through the Sir Syad Ahmad Court to the Salar Manzil, which is the College dining hall, and thence to the science laboratories. Here we had an interesting conversation on the progress of science and the tremendous advance which had taken place in scientific education. From the laboratories we went to the Lytton Library, where the Colonel Sahib and I signed our names in the visitors' book, and thence to the Strachey Hall, the Nizam Museum, and the College Mosque. Before leaving the latter building, which I was sorry to see was still in an unfinished condition, we offered our prayers for the founders and benefactors of the College. We next visited the Collegiate School and the English House. Here Mr. Rees, the Head Master, acted as our guide. After showing us the school, he took us to his class-room, where we heard him teach the tenth class. Before leaving we inspected the boarding-houses both of the College and the school.

In the afternoon, the architect's plans for a new girls' school were brought for my inspection. I had hoped to lay the foundation-stone of this building; but as the ceremony could not take place for some days, I wrote a letter to the College authorities explaining my inability to postpone my departure and urging them to commence building operations with as little delay as possible. Later in the afternoon I was visited by the wife of Nawab Viqar-ul-mulk, and a number of other Muhammadan ladies whose husbands were connected with the College, all of whom I was very glad to meet. I left Aligarh for Bhopal the same evening.

The Hon'ble Colonel Hugh Daly held the post of Agent to the Governor-General in Central India for a period of five years. Twenty-six years previously the same office was held by his father, Sir Henry Daly, whose name is still honoured in Central India as that of a sympathetic, just and skilful administrator. Colonel Daly followed in his father's footsteps, and he will long be remembered with affection and gratitude by all classes of the people.

A British officer always takes a special pride in administering a province or district which was once in his father's or his grandfather's charge. It is natural that he should feel drawn to the people of a locality where his name is already known and respected, and that he should be eager to renew and strengthen the friendly ties of former days. Such appointments are advantageous both to the Government and to the country; and this was never better exemplified than in the case of Colonel Daly's administration of the Central India Agency.

I owe much to Colonel Daly for his wise counsel, and the personal interest he took in all that concerned the welfare of my State and my family. Throughout his connection with Bhopal he displayed towards me the same sympathy and courtesy which characterized the dealings of his distinguished father with my mother and my grandmother.

Before leaving Central India, Colonel Daly was

kind enough to pay a farewell visit to Bhopal. He arrived on August 10th, accompanied by his Personal Assistant, Major Venis-Gordon, and Major Spence, the Political Agent; and other European officers from Sehore, whom I had in vited to meet him, arrived at the same time. A military gymkhana, arranged by Colonel Obaidullah Khan was held in the afternoon, and was followed in the evening by a dinner at the Lal Kothi. Before the party separated, I proposed the health of the guest of the evening in the following words:

"COLONEL DALY, LADIES AND GENTLEMEN,

I am very grateful to you all for accepting my invitation to this dinner, and I specially thank Colonel Daly for so kindly finding time, on the eve of his departure from Central India, to pay one more visit to my State, and thus afford me the sad privilege of bidding him farewell. I have often spoken with pride of the friendship which has existed for so many years between Colonel Daly's family and my own; so that you will easily understand how keen is my regret that he, who has done so much to strengthen that friendship, should be leaving us. This regret will, I know, be shared by all the Chiefs of Central India, who, like myself, bave experienced Colonel Daly's unfailing kindness, and benefited by his wise and sympathetic counsel.

Ladies and Gentlemen, you will agree with me that to spread education and enlightenment where these are most needed is to do humanity the highest possible service. It is no wonder, then, that the name Daly is held in honour in Central India, where it is synonymous with educational progress. When I say that Colonol Daly, by what he has done for education, has followed in the footsteps of Sir Henry Daly, I have said enough, for I could pay him no higher tribute. He will also be remembered for the economic and social progress which has been such a prominent feature of his period of office. Here, too, he has followed in the footsteps of his distinguished father, with whom he will take an honoured place amongst the benefactors of Central India. Greatly as we regret his departure, we are glad to know that he goes to be Resident in the largest State in India. This leads us to hope that the Government has yet higher promotion in store for him. I can assure him that his career will be watched with the greatest interest by the many friends he is leaving behind him.

Though Mrs. Daly is, unfortunately, not with us to-night, I cannot let pass this opportunity of thanking her for her many kindnesses to me, and I ask Colonel Daly to tell her how sincerely we regret her departure, and how sadly we shall miss her. And now, Ladies and Gentlemen, I ask you to drink to the health of my honoured guest, Colonel Hugh Daly, and to join me in wishing him and Mrs. Daly every happiness in the life that lies before them."

In reply to the toast, Colonel Daly said :

" YOUR HIGHNESS,

I cannot find words in which to acknowledge adequately what Your Highness has said.

My frequent visits to Bhopal, several of which have been connected with important events in Your Highness's family, will always remain associated in my mind with the ideal of princely and womanly courtesy, hospitality and sympathetic friendship. The same courtesy, friendship and a most touching confidence have marked Your Highness's relations with me in official matters. I have often had occasion to refer to The marked progress which has been made by the State under Your Highness's rule, and it is pleasant to think that Your Highness is about to proceed to Simla to receive from His Excellency the Viceroy the Insignia of the highest rank in the Indian Orders. It is a melancholy satisfaction to remember that the distinction was bestowed upon Your Highness by the great Monarch who has recently passed away.

Your Highness has alluded to what has been done for the Daly College; but I must repeat, what I have recently said elsewhere, that the re-organisation has been the work of the Chiefs, and that it is with the Chiefs that the future of the College must rest. I know how ready and competent Your Highness is to bear your full share in that work. It is Your Highness who has originated the scheme for placing the coping stone on the system of the Chiefs' Colleges by establishing a University. No one realises better than Your Highness that in a matter of such importance, it is necessary to proceed with caution. But I know that your Highness's scheme will receive the full and sympathetic consideration of the Government of India, and I shall hope to see it launched before I leave the country.

You have referred to social advances in Central India in the last few years. You will permit me to say that, in my opinion, the most notable and happy advance was Your Highness's decision to mingle freely with your guests and friends. I can only hope that it has given Your Highness a tithe of the pleasure which it has given us. It has also proved of solid advantage in many ways. For instance, I well remember that, when Your Highness presided at the first meeting which you attended of the Managing Committee of the Daly College, His Highness the Maharaja Sindhia told me, immediately on his return from the meeting, that on no previous occasion had the proceedings been conducted in so tactful and businesslike a manner.

My wife has specially charged me to assure Your Highness how much she regrets not being able to bid you goodbye in person. I am deeply grateful, as she will be, for what you have so kindly said about her.

Once more congratulating Your Highness on the success

which has attended your able and untiring efforts for the good of your State and people, and once more thanking you for all your kindness and hospitality to me and mine, I will ask your guests to join me in drinking to your long life and prosperity."

CHAPTER X

A VISIT TO SIMLA

On New Year's Day, 1910, I had the honour of being made a G.C.S.I., and in the month of August I attended the investiture ceremony held at Simla by His Excellency, Lord Minto. I left Bhopal on August 23rd, taking with me my three sons, and Sahibzadi Birjis Jahan Begam. We travelled by rail to Khalka, and thence by motor car to Simla. We occupied the house of the Maharaja of Darbhanga, which has a fine situation and beautiful surroundings. The journey proved very fatiguing, and we took two days' complete rest before we set forth to pay calls; and see the sights of Simla.

The first social function to which I was invited was a children's fancy-dress ball at Viceregal Lodge. The Political Agent, my three sons, my three grandchildren, Birjis Jahan Begam, Habibullah Khan and Wahid-uz-zafar Khan, and Munshi Israr Hasan Khan all went to the ball with me. Her Excellency, Lady Minto, received me, and took me to the room in which refreshments were being served, and we had tea with the children. The scene in the ballroom was extremely gay and picturesque. The children were dressed in costumes representing the different nations of the world. Birjis Jahan wore a Turkish dress which was much admired, especially by the European ladies. When the dancing was over, each child was presented to Her Excellency, and received from her a toy or medal which had been specially made for the occasion. My grandsons each received a medal, and Birjis Jahan Begam a kinder-garten drawing box. In thanking Her Excellency for these marks of her kindness I said that I took it as a happy omen that she had decorated my grandsons with her own hand, and I hoped that in days to come their breasts would be covered with medals won in the service of the British Empire. I much enjoyed this fancy-dress ball. It seemed to me an ideal way of entertaining children ; for while it gave them immense pleasure, it had a distinct educative value ; and as I watched the merry faces around me, I thought how fortunate is the lot of children who are brought up in refined homes by cultured mothers.

My investiture took place at Viceregal Lodge. Although the ceremony was private, Lady Minto showed her kind regard for me by inviting nearly a hundred guests to witness the ceremony. I took Muhammad Habibullah Khan and Muhammad Wahid-uz-zafar Khan with me as my pages. On reaching Viceregal Lodge, I was shown into a reception room, where Lady Minto was awaiting my arrival. After a few minutes' conversation, Major Spence, the Political Agent in Bhopal, took me to Mr. G. B. Wood, the officiating Foreign Secretary, who in turn conducted me to the hall of investiture where His Excellency awaited us. He was seated with Lady Minto on a dais, and the members of the Viceregal Staff stood below them on their right. The occasion being a private one, no special arrangements were made for the seating of the guests, and no order of precedence was observed. I entered the hall with Mr. Wood, who, when we had approached to within four paces of the dais, said in a loud voice :

" Your Excellency, I present to Your Excellency Nawab Sultan Jahan Begam, Grand Commander of the Indian Empire, on whom, in January last, His Imperial Majesty King Edward VII conferred the title, Grand Commander of the Star of India." Lord Minto then stood up and decorated me with the cordon and star of the order, at the same time offering me his congratulations. I briefly expressed my gratitude for the honour I had received, and was then invited to take my seat beside their Excellencies.

After the ceremony there was a dance, followed by supper in an adjoining room. I partook of some light refreshment, and after watching the dancing, which was resumed after supper, I bade their Excellencies good-night.

Amongst other social gatherings which I attended

was a purdah party given by Lady Dane, wife of the Lieutenant-Governor of the Punjab, to which the principal European and Indian ladies of Simla were invited. On my arrival I was very kindly received by Lady Dane, and as no other guest had yet put in an appearance, and Sir Louis Dane had expressed a desire to meet me, we went to see him in his own room. I had a pleasant conversation with him, and then returned to the reception room, where the other ladies had by this time assembled. Amongst the many interesting and distinguished ladies I met on this occasion were the Begam and sister of the Nawab Sahib of Maler Kotla, the daughter of the Nawab Sahib of Loharu, the wife of Nawab Muhammad Hayat Khan, Lady Harnam Singh, and Mrs. Sinha. Many English ladies were also present, and the mingling of Eastern and Western costumes made a most pleasing and interesting picture. Tea was served in the drawing-room ; and after tea Lady Minto joined the party. Her Excellency had a kind word for every one. In the case of those who did not understand English, I acted as her interpreter.

I had, before leaving Bhopal, received a letter from the wife of Nawab Zulfiqar Ali Khan in which she wrote that she was anxious to give a party in my honour to the Indian ladies of Simla. She now wrote to me again, reminding me of her desire. But as it was not my intention to make a long stay at Simla, and I had a large number of engagements to fulfil, I replied that it was unfortunately impossible for me to take advantage of her kind proposal. I was sorry to miss this party ; but my regret was lessened by the fact that I had already met most of the Simla ladies at Lady Dane's house. Before my departure, I was visited by the wives of the Nawab Ṣahib of Maler Kotla, and Nawab Zulfiqar Khan, and by Lady Harnam Singh. I returned the call of the first-named lady. I was also invited to tea by Lady Creagh, wife of H. E. the Commander-in-Chief, and by Mrs. Earl, wife of the Home Member. I much regretted that I could not accept Mrs. Earl's invitation, as I was attending a party at Viceregal Lodge on the same afternoon. On my way to the latter, however, I took the opportunity of calling on Mrs. Earl.

I may here mention that it was my good fortune to enjoy fine weather whenever I went out in the afternoon. It seemed to me a most remarkable feature of the Simla climate that whereas the mornings were almost always overclouded and showery, the sky invariably cleared after mid-day, and in the afternoons, when the parties took place, it was fine and dry.

As Colonel Obaidullah Khan was A.D.C. to His Excellency, he was invited to dine at Viceregal Lodge. Though he accepted this invitation, and took part in other social functions, he was still far from well, and I decided to take the opportunity of consulting Surgeon-General Lukis, who was doctor to His Excellency, and one of the most eminent medical men in India. As General Lukis could not see any patients, or engage in any private practice, without special permission, I wrote to Colonel Pinhey, His Excellency's Private Secretary, explaining my desire, and he at once obtained for me the necessary sanction. General Lukis then saw my son, and, after a careful examination, assured me that his malady was not of a dangerous description. This greatly cheered me; and my anxiety was still further diminished when a day or two later Their Excellencies told me that General Lukis had spoken very hopefully of my son's condition.

My little grandchild, Birjis Jahan Begam, to show how much she appreciated the paint-box which Lady Minto had given to her at the children's party, painted a bunch of grapes on a sachet, and sent it to Her Excellency, together with her photograph and a letter in her own handwriting. On another occasion when she accompanied me to Viceregal Lodge she recited some verses about a butterfly which pleased Lady Minto very much. "You have recited very nicely," she said, and added "I never see and butterflies here," Birjis Jahan remembered her words, and, when she got home she painted a butterfly, and sent it to Lady Eileen Elliot with a letter in which she wrote, "Please show this to Her Excellency, and say from me 'Here is a butterfly for you.'" Lady Eileen wrote back saying that Her Excellency was delighted with the butterfly.

Colonel Obaidullah Khan, who found the hill climate very trying, left Simla two days before me. The Nawab Sahib and his family left at the same time. My own departure took place on September 5th. I called on Mr. Wood in the morning, and then proceeded by motor car to Khalka. I had thought to break my journey at Delhi ; but, as I was feeling tired after the busy days I had spent at Simla, and as the month of Ramazan was close at hand, I decided to travel straight home. Moreover, my arrival at Bhopal was to be public ; and as the date had already been fixed, I did not care to change it. Sahibzada Hamidullah Khan had made arrangements for a special train to be in readiness for us at Khalka. To this my saloon was attached, and we continued our journey without delay, reaching Bhopal at 3 p.m. on September 6th. All the officials and Khans of the State came to receive me at the railway station, which had been grandly decorated in honour of my arrival. Rain had fallen that morning, and was followed during the next two or three days by heavy showers, which were very beneficial to the crops.

CHAPTER XI

CLOSING EVENTS OF THE YEAR 1911

SHORTLY after my return from Simla, Mr. M. F. O'Dwyer, who had succeeded Colonel Daly as Agent to the Governor-General in Central India, paid his first official visit to Bhopal. He arrived at 11-30 a.m. on the 19th of October, accompanied by Mr. D. Gabriel, his First Assistant, and Captain Harvey, his Personal Assistant. His arrival was public, and all the formalities proper to the occasion were observed. At 1 p.m., in accordance with a pre-arranged programme, he paid a formal visit to me at the Sadar Manzil palace. He was attended by the Political Agent, his First and Personal Assistants, and the Mir Munshi of the Indore Residency. At 3 p.m., accompanied by my three sons, I paid the return visit.

The next morning, His Honour went to see the archæological remains at Sanchi. He returned to Bhopal at midday, and in the afternoon received visits from the Muin-ul-muham, the Nasir-ul-muham, and a number of the leading *jagirdars*. On the morning of the 20th, he visited the Alexandra and Jahangiria High Schools, the Prince of Wales Hospital, the Museum, and the lines of the Victoria Lancers. In the afternoon he witnessed a gymkhana, specially arranged in his honour by Colonel Obaidullah Khan. Numerous other guests were invited to the gymkhana, and also to a banquet which took place the same evening at the Lal Kothi. At the banquet, I made a short speech in which I proposed Mr. O'Dwyer's health, and expressed the great pleasure which it gave me to welcome him to my State.

In responding to the toast, Mr. O'Dwyer said :

"Your Highness, Ladies and Gentlemen,

"I thank Your Highness very sincerely for the kindly and graceful terms in which you have proposed the toast of my health, and I thank you, Ladies and Gentlemen, for the cordial manner in which you have received it. Coming as a stranger to Bhopal, I appreciate very warmly the welcome with which Your Highness has greeted me, and the hospitality which I have experienced here as Your Highness's guest.

"It has been a great pleasure and a privilege to make the acquaintance of a ruler whose fame has extended all over the Indian Empire, and to have the opportunity of seeing the picturesque city with its beautiful environment, which Your Highness's public spirit and good taste have done so much to embellish and adorn.

"I am glad to hear from Your Highness that there is promise of a bountiful harvest, and trust that a continuance of good seasons will soon make good the gap caused by the famine of 10 years ago. From what Your Highness has told me I also gather that the finances of the State are steadily improving, and that the State administration, under the skilful direction of your Revenue and Judicial Ministers and Your Highness's rigorous control, is being carried on with firmness and ability.

"It has been a great pleasure to me that, on this my first visit to Bhopal, I have been privileged to present to Your Highness the Warrant of the Order of the G.C.S.I. with the insignia of which Your Highness was invested by His Excellency the Viceroy at Simla last month—and to congratulate Your Highness on this great but well merited accession of dignity bestowed by His Illustrious Majesty the late King-Emperor in recognition of Your Highness's tried loyalty to the Government, your steady devotion to duty, and unflagging zeal in all matters of public interest and public improvement. These are qualities for which the Begams of Bhopal have been conspicuous for nearly a century; but which Your Highness has developed to an extent which it would be difficult to parallel and still more difficult to surpass. Ladies and Gentlemen, I ask you to join with me in drinking the health of Her Highness and in wishing that her wise and beneficent rule may be prolonged for many happy years, to be a powerful support to the Government and a source of prosperity and contentment to her people."

After my health had been drunk, I bade Mr. O'Dwyer goodbye, as he had made arrangements to leave Bhopal that night.

I had been looking forward to meeting Mr. O'Dwyer at Indore in November, and also to attending the Council Meeting to be held at the Daly College on the 12th of the month; but my plans were unfortunately frustrated. At this Council Meeting my pamphlets on the education of Indian Chiefs, which I had submitted in November 1908 and April 1909, were to be discussed, and I was, therefore, particularly anxious to be present. I found, however, that it would be impossible for me to be at Indore on the appointed date; so I wrote a fresh note in support of my views, and entrusted it to my Revenue Minister, who attended the meeting as my representative.

In this note I again emphasized the need for a separate university for the sons of Chiefs, and at the same time urged the introduction of a higher standard of education in the existing Chiefs Colleges, as a necessary preliminary to the establishment of a university. I have given years of thought to these matters, and have discussed them with many educational experts, and I am thoroughly convinced that if any real advance is to be made in the training of Indian Chiefs, it can only be on the lines I have so often indicated.

The Muin-ul-muham put my note before the meeting, and it was unanimously agreed that the existing courses of study were in need of revision. It was also resolved that I should be asked to submit my recommendations in regard thereto for consideration at a future meeting of the council.

On the 22nd November, I went to Bombay to bid farewell to Lord and Lady Minto. Colonel Obaidullah Khan had an attack of fever, and was unable to make the journey; but my eldest and youngest sons accompanied me. We reached Bombay in the morning, and the same day we met and said goodbye to Their Excellencies on the Apollo Bunder. I presented them with my photograph, and a copy of my book, the *Tuzuk-i-Sultani*.

The reader does not need to be reminded of the ability and wisdom with which Lord Minto administered the affairs of this country. His sympathy with all classes of the people, from the prince to the peasant, his unvarying courtesy and geniality, and his countless acts of kindness, the bare enumeration of which would fill a volume will long be held in grateful remembrance. Both as a statesman, and on account of his high personal qualities Lord Minto is entitled to rank among the greatest of Indian Viceroys.

It was just at this time that a decision was reached as to the manner in which Central India should perpetuate the memory of King Edward VII, to whom the people, and particularly the Chiefs of the Agency, had been so deeply attached. The subject was one of those which were discussed at the Daly College Council meeting to which I have referred above. A short time previously I had received a letter from His Highness the Maharaja Sahib of Sailana asking me whether I favoured the idea of the erection of a statue of His late Majesty. In reply I said I thought the memorial should be of a kind that would confer some permanent boon on the people of the country ; and I suggested, instead of a statue, the founding of an orphanage, or home for destitute and fatherless children. This suggestion was put before the Council meeting, and with it another made by Colonel Roberts and Mr. Drake Brockman, that the funds collected should be devoted to the establishment of a home for patients suffering from tuberculosis. The latter idea appealed very strongly to me, and as it accorded with my views that the memorial should supply a public need, I withdrew my own proposal, and Colonel Roberts' scheme was approved. I gave a donation of Rs. 10,000 towards the Home, and promised to contribute Rs. 100 a month towards its maintenance. I also informed the Memorial Committee that if Bhopal should be considered a suitable locality for the Home, I should be glad to provide a site on a hill to the north of the city, where the air is pure and the climate salubrious. I am confident that when this Home is established, whether in Bhopal or elsewhere, it will be an immense blessing to the people of Central India. It will at the same time be a worthy and fitting memorial of our late beloved King.

In the month of December I went to Allahabad to see the Industrial Exhibition then being held in that city. I had received a special invitation to visit the exhibition from Sir John Hewett, the Lieutenant-Governor of the Urthed Provinces, who was its principal organizer ; and my desire to see it had been increased by the accounts I had read of it in the newspapers. I took only a small staff with me to Allahabad, and stayed in my own camp, which was pitched close to Government House.

I inspected every part of the exhibition, devoting special attention to the agricultural section, in which I was gready interested, and to the Ladies' court. In the latter, some of my own embroidery was on view, as well as some needle-work done by Birjis Jahan Begam and Shah Bano Begam.

By organizing this exhibition, Sir John Hewett did a great service to the United Provinces, and it is to be hoped that his example will be followed by the administrators of other provinces. For exhibitions of this nature help to enlighten and educate the public mind, and to provide the stimulus and encouragement which the indigenous arts and industries of India so badly need.

At Allahabad I made the acquaintance of many European and Indian ladies and gentlemen. Amongst these was the Aga Khan, with whom I had a long talk on the subject of the Moslem university. I subsequently gave a lakh of rupees to the university fund. I also met and received much kindness and hospitality from Mr. Porter, the Commissioner of Allahabad, and his wife, and also from Lady Stanley. Mrs. Porter invited me to tea in the Ladies' court of the Exhibition. Here I met the Maharani of Vizianagram, the Begam Sahiba of Janjira, who was a very old friend of mine, and the daughter of Shamsher Jung. Mrs. Crosthwaite, the daughter-in-law of the Resident at Indore, who has a very sweet voice, entertained us with songs, and Miss Atia Fyzee sang a hymn in praise of the Holy Prophet. On the following day I went to an 'At Home' at the house of the Commissioner. On this occasion Mrs. Porter presented me with a silver box inlaid with amethysts, and on which were engraved some sentences from the

Quran. She said that she had had the box for many years, and had always kept it with great reverence. "I should like you to have it," she said, "because it is inscribed with words from the Holy Book of the Mussalmans." I thanked her very much, and said I should greatly value the box. She next presented gifts to the Maharani of Vizianagram, and the daughter of Shamsher Jung, after which she took us all to the Exhibition to see the court of Forestry. I had very much wished to see this court, but had been unable to do so previously owing to the great crowd of people. Mrs. Porter very kindly made arrangements so that I could visit the Exhibition between 8 and 10 o'clock in the morning, and the attendant in charge of each court was instructed to be present between those hours and act as my guide. In this way I was able to see everything with great comfort, as the general public were not admitted before 11 o'clock.

Before setting out for Allahabad, I had received a telegram from the Rani of Partabgarh, whom I had met at Mussoorie, to say that she proposed to form an Association which was to have for its object the improvement of the lives of Indian women. She requested me to be president of the Association, and added that she hoped that Queen Alexandra would consent to become its patroness. I asked her to send me further details of her proposal, which she did ; and I then wrote and said I should be glad to become a member of the Association, but I declined, on the ground of my heavy work as a ruler, the office of president, as I felt that this could suitably be left to some other Begam or Maharani with more leisure at her disposal. Ultimately, the Begam Sahiba of Janjira was elected president, and I attended the first meeting of the Association, which took place at Allahabad before I left. The Begam Sahiba came to my camp to conduct me to the meeting, which was well attended. Amongst those present were Mrs. Sarala Devi Chowdhrani, the Secretary, Miss Sorabji, and several European ladies. After the usual preliminaries, the Secretary explained the purpose of the Maha Mandal Sabha, as the new Association had been named. Miss Sorabji and other ladies, both Indian and European, then addressed the meeting. All these ladies spoke very well ; but as they used the English language, which the majority of their listeners did not understand, their eloquence was to a large extent wasted. I had not intended to speak ; but it seemed to me that, before asking the audience for an expression of approval or disapproval, it would be as well for someone to explain to them what the meeting was about. I therefore stood up and gave in Urdu a résume of the Secretary's address and the remarks made by the other speakers. I regard speeches in English as altogether out of place on occasions of this description. Their only effect is to weary the audience, and reduce the attendance at subsequent meetings. English ladies who are kind enough to address gatherings of their Indian sisters must of course do so in the English language; but their speeches should in every case be translated as soon as they have been delivered.

CHAPTER XII

I ENTERTAIN MY FRIENDS

In the month of February, 1911, I invited a number of my European friends to Bhopal to take part in the festivities which were to be held in honour of my having been made a G.C.S.I. Both the Agent to the Governor-General for Central India, and the Chief Commissioner for the Central Provinces accepted my invitation, and other friends came from Indore, Hoshangabad, Sehore, Jhansi, and Nagpur. They all arrived on February 14th, and were accommodated at the Lal Kothi and the Guest House, and in two large camps pitched for the occasion. The catering arrangements were carried out by the manager of a large hotel in Lucknow. My friends stayed three days at Bhopal, and were entertained in various ways in accordance with a previously arranged programme.

On the morning of the 16th, the last and busiest day, Mr. O'Dwyer and most of the other guests visited the Alexandra and Jahangiria High Schools, and the Edward Museum. Breakfast followed; after which I took my lady guests to the Sultania School, the Victoria School, and the Princess of Wales Club. We reached the Sultania School, where I was to preside at a prize distribution, at 11 o'clock. As soon as we had taken our places in the school-room, the students and teachers together sang the Bhopal national hymn. A number of girls who had completed the reading of the Quran were then presented to me. They recited some verses from the Holy Book, and I gave each of them, and also their teacher, a *sari*. After this little ceremony the Lady Superintendent read a report on the progress of the school, on the conclusion of which I rose and said : " I have listened to the report which has just been read with much pleasure ; for nothing gives me greater satisfaction than the knowledge that my people are progressing in education. Culture is the basis of civilization, and female education is the key to culture. I congratulate Mrs. Bakhsh on the steady progress which this school has made under her energetic and skilful management. I am glad to have this opportunity of acknowledging the valuable work she has done, and I assure her that her efforts will continue to receive my support and assistance. I have been greatly encouraged by the remarks which my European friends have made after inspecting the schools of Bhopal. I am sure that the Sultania School will continue to deserve their high opinions, and that I shall always have reason to be proud of the good work and behaviour of my girl students.

I was very pleased to read the essay written by Kulsum Bai, and I hope to receive similar proofs of progress from other students. I am also glad to see that you are paying attention to painting and needle-work, and I congratulate Mrs. Bakhsh and her staff on the distinctions won by their pupils at the Lahore and Nagpur exhibitions.

And now, my daughters, let me ask you to make the most of the opportunities that have been given you. Seek diligently to acquire knowledge, which is a woman's wealth, and culture, which is her adornment; but do not forget that true comeliness consists in nobility of character. In this way you will grow up to be loved by old and young: misfortunes will be unable to crush you, and worldly prosperity will never make you proud. Remember that the object of your education is not that you may undertake the duties of men; but that you may acquire those womanly accomplishments and virtues which will enable you to become capable housewives and good mothers. The management of a home and the training of a child are two of the noblest and most responsible of human duties, and God created woman for their performance." My speech was followed by the prize distribution, and the proceedings closed with the singing of the national anthem.

Our next visit was to the Victoria School which had recently been transferred from its old premises to a more commodious building in Shahjahanabad. Miss Rudra, a trained lady teacher, was in charge of this institution, which had made great improvement under her management. After showing us over the building, which had been decorated in honour of our visit, Miss Rudra read an address of welcome, which I acknowledged by a few brief remarks. I had not expected an address here, and so had not come prepared to make a speech. This was, however, just as well, as our time was getting short. From the school we went to the Ladies' Club. We had a hearty reception from the members, and stayed at the Club till one o'clock.

A gymkhana, in which several of my guests were competitors, occupied the afternoon, and in the evening there was a State dinner at the Lal Kothi. At the dinner, which I attended with my sons and my two chief ministers, the Muin-ul-muham and the Nasir-ul-muham, I made the following speech :—

" MR. O'DWYER, LADIES AND GENTLEMEN,

I thank you all most heartily for the kindness and honour you have done me in coming to take part with me in celebrating the honour which was bestowed on me last year by His Majesty the King-Emperor, and the insignia of which were presented to me at Simla this year by His Majesty's Viceroy, Lord Minto. I am very sensible of the honour His Majesty had done me in creating me a Grand Commander of the Star of India, and, Ladies and Gentlemen, it will always be a matter of pride to me that I was decorated with the emblems of this high Order by one of the most distinguished

Viceroys who have ever presided over the destinies of India. You will, I know, agree with me that Lord Minto's administrative policy was as remarkable for its wisdom as for its success. Equally remarkable were the courage, the tact, and the self-possession which he invariably displayed in the face of difficulties and dangers. I am myself firmly convinced that no policy was better suited to the crisis through which India was then passing, or more likely to lead to the restoration of tranquillity, than that which Lord Minto pursued. But in addition to his great services, Lord Minto will be remembered for his personal qualities, his urbanity, his kindly nature, and his never-failing sympathy. It is for these qualities, and more than all for his wide sympathy, that his name is cherished not only by those who, like myself, enjoyed the privilege of his friendship, but by all classes and sections of the people. For, Ladies and Gentlemen, there is nothing which India needs more, and nothing which she appreciates more highly, than sympathy. I have not yet had the privilege of meeting Lord Hardinge; but his high reputation and the valuable services he has rendered the Empire in numerous important posts, encourages us to believe that the administration of our country and the interest of her peoples are as safe in his hands as in those of his predecessor.

Before passing on to other subjects, I cannot help referring to the glad tidings we have received that His Majesty the King-Emperor is shortly, and for the second time in his life, to visit this country. The prospect of welcoming and paying homage to their beloved Sovereign has given untold joy to his Indian subjects. They have never forgotten how, on that historic occasion at the Guildhall, after his first visit to the East, he urged his hearers to ever to bear in mind that India must be ruled with sympathy; and from that day to this they have yielded him unquestioning devotion. By his readiness to undertake this long journey, His Majesty gives us yet another proof of his affection for his Indian subjects, and his solicitation for their welfare.

And now, Ladies and Gentlemen, I desire, with your permission, to say a few words about the administration of my State. You will be glad to know that excellent progress continues to be made in the Land Revenue Department. Cultivators are now beginning to take a real interest in the improvement and development of their holdings, and *mustajirs* are learning that by taking thought for the future they can make both themselves and the villages under their charge more prosperous. You will also be glad to hear that the arrears of revenue due to the State, the accumulation of years, have now been finally disposed of. Of the large sum outstanding, as much as possible was collected, and the remainder, amounting to thirty-eight lakhs of rupees, was cancelled. I may add that since the introduction of the new settlement there has not been a single case of non-payment, a sure sign of the improved condition of both cultivators and *mustajirs*. It was with the desire of promoting the welfare of my people—a duty incumbent on every Ruler—that I decided to visit the Allahabad exhibition. I was greatly interested in all that I saw at the exhibition, and especially in the agricultural section, where I spent much time. I also purchased several agricultural implements which will be sent to Bhopal as soon as the exhibition closes. These it is my intention to display in different parts of the State, so that my people may see them in use, and each may learn something of the improvement that is possible in his own branch of cultivation. The judicial and police departments continue to maintain their reputation for efficiency. I am satisfied that in all my courts justice is administered, and I am glad to say that throughout my territory order and tranquillity prevail, and that the loyalty of my people to the British throne and to their Ruler is as strong to-day as it has always been in the past. I was much gratified to learn from Lord Minto, during his recent visit to Bhopal, that the Government has acceded to my request, made some years ago, that in consideration of the hereditary loyalty of my State, I may increase the establishment of Imperial Service Troops which I maintain. I have not yet received the Government's formal sanction; but judging from the manner in which Lord Minto spoke, this should reach me very shortly. The increased efficiency of my army is a great satisfaction to me, and I trust that the marked progress of the past few years will continue. I am also well satisfied with the work of the educational department, now one of the most important branches of the administration. I am especially pleased with the progress that has been made by the Sultania Girls' School. This year four girls are to appear for the middle-school examination of the Allahabad University. This is the first time that girls from Bhopal have been sent up for a University examination. Increased attention is now being paid to the industrial side of the school, and highly creditable results are being achieved. At the Arts exhibitions recently held at Nagpore and Lahore, several girls were awarded medals, and examples of the work done at the school are now being shown at the Allahabad exhibition. Ladies and Gentlemen, I need not take up any more of your time. I again thank you all most cordially for your kindness in coming to take part in these festivities, and in conclusion, I ask you to drink to the health of my honoured guests, Mr. and Mrs. O'Dwyer."

In replying to the toast Mr. O'Dwyer said:

"YOUR HIGHNESS, LADIES AND GENTLEMEN,

I am very grateful to Your Highness for having so kindly proposed my wife's health and mine, and I thank you, Ladies and Gentlemen, for your cordial reception of the toast.

We have listened with the greatest interest to the eloquent words in which Her Highness has indicated her view of her duties as Ruler, and her description of how she has discharged them. Those duties are twofold: loyalty and attachment to the Throne and Government, and the obligation to work for the well being and improvement of the people. In both respects Her Highness has set a brilliant example to the whole Indian Empire. In every branch of the administration she has shown the keenest solicitude for her people, and it is to her personal efforts, ably supported by her sons, Nawab Nasrullah Khan and Sahibzada Obaidullah Khan, and by her two capable Ministers whom we are glad to see here this evening, that sound progress has been achieved during her ten years' rule in so many directions. The revenue administration has been improved, the Judicial and Police Departments have been reformed, and I am glad to hear from my old friend, Mr. Laurie, the Commissioner of the Narbada Division, how much has been done to repress dacoity along the border, and how effectively the State Police have co-operated with those of the neighbouring British districts in the prevention and detection of crime. At the same time steady efforts are being made to extend medical relief to all classes; and as regards education we have, through Her Highness's kindness, had an opportunity of seeing with our own eyes the admirable institutions for the education of boys and girls which she has established, and the excellent results that have already been attained.

Ladies and Gentlemen, the record which I have briefly sketched is one of which any ruler in the East or West might well be proud. But Her Highness is not content to rest on her laurels, or to limit her energies to the advancement of her own people. She is foremost in initiating or assisting every project for the public good even outside her State, and we have had a notable illustration of this in the moral and material support she has just given to the scheme for creating in India a Muhammadan University, a scheme which now appears likely to be realised, and which, when established on a sound basis, will we trust, give India an institution which will revive the glories of Granada and Cordova. How Her Highness has discharged her obligation to the Throne and the British Government, it is unnecessary for me to state. The loyalty of the Bhopal Chiefs is proverbial and has been consecrated by a 100 years of unswerving fidelity.

Ladies and Gentlemen, you have doubtless heard of the splendid services rendered to the British Government by Her Highness's illustrious ancestress, the Sikandar Begam, in the dark days of the Mutiny. But it may be interesting to recall the memorable words, in which those services were acknowledged by the then Viceroy, Lord Canning. At a Durbar specially convened at Jabalpur in 1861, His Excellency addressed Her Highness the Sikandar Begam in the following words: 'Your Highness is very welcome to this Durbar. I have long desired to thank you for the services you have rendered to the British Government. Your Highness is the Ruler of a State which is conspicuous in history for never having been in arms against the British power; and lately when that State was beset and threatened by our enemies, you, a woman, guided its affairs with a courage, an ability, and a success which would have done honour to any statesman or soldier.

Her Highness has worthily carried on the grand traditions, to which she has succeeded. She, too, a woman, has ruled her State with a courage, an ability and a success which would have done credit to any statesman; and if the occasion arose, she would, I am confident, show equal capacity as a soldier. This is proved by Her Highness's loyal desire to put all the forces of her State at the disposal of the Imperial Government; and those who are competent to judge are aware that her Imperial Service Troops have been worked up, by the unremitting efforts of her son, Colonel Obaidullah Khan, to a pitch of efficiency which has made them a most valuable force in the scheme of imperial defence. The loyal and ready assistance of the Sikandar Begam at the grave crisis of the Mutiny was rewarded with the grant of a considerable slice of territory, and it is a subject of great delight and gratification to her many friends that Her Highness's noble work has not gone unrecognised, and that last year she was honoured by the late King-Emperor with the title of G.C.S.I., perhaps the highest distinction attainable in this great Empire of India; and I am sure it is a great pleasure to us all to meet here as Her Highness's guests to celebrate this happy event.

Your Highness, I fear I have taken up much of your time, but before I sit down I have one duty to discharge, namely, to thank you on behalf of all your guests for your splendid hospitality, and for the solicitude you have shown in making our stay here an interesting and pleasant one. I am sure we shall all carry away a delightful recollection of Bhopal, of its noble palaces, stately mosques, shady gardens and picturesque lake. But we shall carry away an even brighter memory of our warm-hearted hostess and her charming family, of whom I must not forget to mention Your Highness's dear little grand-daughter, Birjis Jahan Begam, whose *nashra* is one of the occasions of this gathering.

Ladies and Gentlemen, Her Highness has adorned many spheres and won many distinctions; but I am sure you will agree with me that in one sphere, namely, as a hostess, she is without a peer or a rival. I now ask you to drink to the health of our hostess, and to join with me in wishing that she may long be spared to work for the good of her people, to enjoy her well-earned honours, and to win further distinction in a career which has been among the most brilliant and remarkable in our time."

After the speeches, there was a display of fireworks. This brought the festivities to an end, and my guests departed the following morning.

On the 22nd February, I celebrated the *nashra* of Birjis Jahan Begam. This ceremony, which is performed when a child has completed the reading of the Holy Quran, took place at the Sadar Manzil palace, and all the ladies of my family, and the wives of the leading State officials and gentry of the town, were invited to witness it. The ceremony, a very simple one, consisted in my bestowing on Birjis Jahan Begam, the heroine of the occasion, a robe of honour and decorating her with jewels. Having thus adorned her in the presence of the assembled ladies, I presented robes of honour first to my three daughters-in-law, and then to the ladies of my family, and to the wives of certain of the higher officials. At a second gathering, which took place later, I distributed robes to the other ladies who had attended the ceremony, and also to my dependants and servants.

CHAPTER XIII

SOME MORE ADMINISTRATIVE REFORMS

VISITORS to the city of Bhopal always remark on the beauty of the surrounding scenery. Magnificent views are obtainable from the principal buildings and from many of the main roads. I have always taken a special delight in adding to the attractions of my capital ; and by judicious demolitions, pulling down an unsightly house here or lowering a wall there, I have been able to open up many pleasing vistas. This year, I lowered to half its height the long wall which forms the southern boundary of Shahjahanabad ; and the traveller who approaches the city from the north now sees on his left laand, instead of a blank wall, an extensive landscape stretching far away to the blue eastern hills, with the beautiful Benazir and Taj Mahal palaces, and their adjoining lakes, in the foreground. Seen in the early morning, or in the light of The setting sun, this view is very entrancing. The completion of the new Alexandra High School, and the laying out of a public garden, have still further improved this entrance to the city. Other buildings under construction are the Courts of Justice, the Revenue

Court, the Public Library, the Qiran-us-sadain on the hill near the Idgah, and new bungalows for the State Engineer and the Lady Doctor. Under the head of Public Works, must be included the extension of the water supply. The original water-works were erected by the Nawab Qudsia Begam at her own cost, and are still in use. But the population of Bhopal is now far larger than it was in the days of the Qudsia Begam, and much more water is needed than the old works could provide. I accordingly installed two new pumping engines, one for supplying water to Ahmedabad, which has already grown into a small town, and the other, erected at Karbala, to supply that portion of the city which lies without the Imami Gate, and the adjacent parts of Shahjahanabad.

In the land revenue administration some important changes were made. I have already mentioned that when the 19 years' settlement was introduced, there were certain villages which could not be brought under its operation because they had been settled for a period of 30 years, and this period had not yet expired. It was now enacted that, in the event of a *mustajir* of this district showing himself to be unfit for his position, his village should be taken away from him, and re-settled under the 19 years' system. I also at this time abolished the Piklon *tahsil*, which had been administered on special lines, and incorporated it with the neighbouring *tahsil* of Diwangang. In Piklon I had introduced by way of experiment the *ryatwari* system ; but the results were not such as to justify its continuance. I had fixed the assessment very low : so low that the revenue from the eleven villages of the *tahsil*, which had previously amounted to Rs. 27,851 dropped to Rs. 7,676. But the cultivators made no efforts to improve the land. Many took advantage of the low assessment to sublet their holdings to the *mustajirs* of neighbouring districts, while good lands were allowed to lie fallow, the holders finding that they could still make a livelihood by selling the grass and timber that grew upon them. These and other defects of the *ryatwari* tenure convinced me of its unsuitability; and I accordingly extended the 19 years' settlement to the Piklon villages, and placed them under the *mustajiri* system. The revenue was assessed at Rs. 11,697, which the people gladly accepted. Subsequently I found that the disestablishment of the Piklon *tahsil* was a mistake. Piklon is a long way from Diwangang, and the journey to and fro put both *mustajirs* and the officers of the *tahsil* to much expense and inconvenience. I, therefore, decided to re-establish the *tahsil*, and this was done in the course of the year.

The satisfactory working of the new settlement was amply demonstrated by the revenue returns for the year. For the first time in the history of the State, not a single *mustajir* was behindhand in his payments, while no less than 144,765 *bighas* of new land had been brought under cultivation.

The number of persons engaged in agricultural work was also much larger than in previous years, the Western District alone showing an increase of over two thousand cultivators. Providence in his mercy sent us abundant and seasonable rains, and crops everywhere were good.

The condition of the *jagirdars* showed but few signs of improvement. Those who resided in the city had bestirred themselves to the extent of sending their sons to the Alexandra School ; but those in the *mufassil* displayed no inclination to avail themselves of the educational, or indeed of any other opportunities, that were put before them. An exception must, however, be made of the *jagirdars* belonging to, or related to my own family. Amongst these there was a perceptible desire to march with the times. They had begun to take a lively interest in education, and some of them already held official posts, and were doing their best to make themselves capable servants of the State. In the *pargannas* of Berasia and Nazirabad there are a certain number of *jagirdars* of Rajput descent, and amongst them, too, signs of progress were visible. This was mainly due to the establishment in these *pargannas* of a branch of the Hit Karini Sabha, a society which endeavours, by discouraging extravagance and foolish customs and superstitions, to improve the mode of life and the prospects of the Rajput people. This branch of the Sabha is maintained by Thakur Laran Singh at his own expense. I am very grateful to him for the valuable service he has thereby rendered me. The *Jagirdars* of Bhopal occupy, as I have before remarked, a very important position; for, in a country where agriculture is the chief industry, the welfare of the people is to a large degree in the hands of the land-holding class. I have done, and shall continue to do, all that lies in my power for the advancement and enlightenment of this class of my subjects. A set of regulations for the better management of their estates is at the present time under preparation, and will, I hope, shortly be issued.

Advances to cultivators under the *taqavi* system were made during the year with beneficial results. The money advanced was spent on the land, and cultivators increased the value of their holding by improved methods of irrigation and in other ways. Very little progress was made either with the experimental farms, or with the sugar factory at Ichawar; and as neither of these experiments seemed likely to produce useful results, they were discontinued.

The year was marked by steady progress in education. In accordance with an arrangement made with the Government of India, Mr. Mitchell, the Inspector of Schools for the Narbada Division, visited the English schools of the State. In the course of his inspection he made many valuable suggestions, and I was greatly helped by his advice. Nothing gives me greater satisfaction than the knowledge that education is making headway amongst my people. It was, therefore, a very real pleasure to me to learn from Maulavi Syad-ud-din, the Nazim of the Western District, that the people of Ashta had, at his suggestion, but without any pressure being brought to bear on them, collected sufficient money to establish a school for the teaching of English. The school was named the Hamidia School, after my youngest son, Sahibzada Hamidullah Khan; and as soon as it had been opened a further sum of Rs. 300 was raised for its equipment.

A kindergarten class for the training of young children was opened this year in Bhopal. The class was held in the Ali Manzil, and was placed under the superintendence of Miss Rudra, who is a qualified exponent of this form of instruction. The kindergarten system has been in use for many years in European countries, where its advantages have been fully recognized. It is an admirable system for the training of the young, as it imposes no strain on mind or body. The senses are trained, and the mind is developed by means of games and pleasant exercises, so that a child looks upon his lesson as a recreation rather than a task. Unfortunately there are as yet no kindergarten text-books in the Urdu language; so that Mohammadan children are unable to reap the full benefit of this excellent system.

CHAPTER XIV

MY FIRST VISIT TO EUROPE

THE complete story of my first visit to Europe has been admirably told by my beloved Shah Bano Begam, and has been published under the title *Siyahat-i-Sultani*. I shall, therefore, describe my travels as briefly as possible, referring the reader to the *Siyahat-i-Sultani* for fuller details.

I had long ago made up my mind that, as soon as I had set the affairs of my State in order, I would go to Europe, and thereby not only fulfil the Prophet's injunction to "see the world," but gain experience which I should be able to utilize for the benefit of my subjects. It was also my desire to present myself before His Majesty the King-Emperor and his royal Consort, and personally express my loyalty to their persons, and my devotion to the British throne.

With the help of the Almighty I had now carried out what seemed to me the most urgent reforms in the administration of my State. I had devoted ten strenuous years to this work; and, as the various departments of the State were now in good working order, I felt that the opportunity had arrived for fulfilling my long cherished wish. I lost no time in making my preparations; for I was eager to reach London in time to witness His Majesty's Coronation, which was to take place in the month of June.

The male members of my party were Colonel Obaidullah Khan, Sahibzada Hamidullah Khan, Sahibzada Wahid-uz-zafar Khan, Munshi Israr Hasan Khan, Mr. Abdur Samad, Munshi Liaqat Ali, and my Private Secretary, Mr. Wali Muhammad. The ladies who accompanied me were the Shahriar Dulhan, Shah Bano Begam Birjis Jahan Begam, Mrs. Barnes, and Mrs. Bakhsh. My eldest son, Nawab Nasrullah Khan was left in charge of the State during my absence.

We left Bhopal at 7 a.m. on April 7th, and the same evening we embarked at Bombay on s.s *Caledonia*. At Port Said the King and Queen of the Belgians joined our ship. I was introduced to them, and had a long and interesting conversation with the Queen, who is a very charming and cultured lady. We disembarked at Marseilles, and, after a drive round the city in motor cars, left by special train for Paris, where we were to break our journey. On arrival we drove to the Hotel Majestic, where rooms had been engaged for us. During our stay in the French capital we visited the principal picture galleries, the cathedral of Notre Dame, the Bois de Bologne, the Hotel des Invalids, and other places of interest. We also went to Versailles and Fontainbleau.

It had been arranged that, before proceeding to England, we should go to Nauheim in Germany. This town is famous for its salubrious climate, and its mineral springs, and invalids from all parts of the world go there for the sake of the baths. We had engaged a house there, and Colonel Obaidullah Khan had already gone on in advance, when I received information from Colonel Dunlop Smith that His Majesty had expressed his desire that I should attend the levee which he was about to hold. I, therefore, started at once for London, taking Sahibzada Hamidullah Khan with me, and leaving the rest of the party to proceed to Nauheim.

At Dover we were met by Colonel Dunlop Smith, who brought us greetings from His Majesty and the Queen. Their Majesties, he said, were anxious to know that we were none the worse for our long journey, and that I had suffered no serious discomfort during the voyage, or in crossing the Channel. I requested Colonel Dunlop Smith to convey my loyal greetings to Their Majesties, and to tell them that because I was on my way to attend the Coronation of my Sovereign, the elements had been kind and hospitable to me, and that, by God's grace, I had suffered no inconvenience of any kind during either the voyage to Marseilles, or the Channel crossing. From Dover we travelled by special train to

Redhill, where a house had been engaged for us by Messrs. Thos. Cook & Sons. We were very comfortable at Redhill. Our house, which was called Pattison Court, was commodious and fully furnished. The grounds, though small, were beautiful and secluded, so that we were able to take pleasant walks without being seen. The residents of Redhill were very kind and friendly. On the day of our arrival they decorated their houses to welcome us, and throughout our stay they showed us much consideration.

As the levee was to be in the evening we decided to stay in London for the night, and took rooms at St. Ermine's Hotel. At 8 p.m. Colonel Dunlop Smith came to the hotel and took me to Buckingham Palace. Hamidullah Khan accompanied me as my A. D. C. The palace is a magnificent and stately building, and the scene as we entered was one of extraordinary grandeur. We were shown into a large hall adjoining the royal apartments. After a few moments, a court official entered and informed Colonel Dunlop Smith that His Majesty was ready to receive me, and we followed him into the royal presence. Their Majesties came forward to meet us, and shook hands first with me and then with Hamidullah Khan. His Majesty graciously enquired about my health and my journey to England, and then asked after the health of Colonel Obaidullah Khan. On hearing that he was at Nauheim, he enquired if it was his intention to come to England. I replied that he would come to England shortly. The Queen was also kind enough to talk to me for a few minutes, and then the private audience came to an end. I was now conducted to the Throne Room. Here were assembled the members of the royal family, the nobles of the Empire, the Ministers of State, and the ambassadors of foreign Powers. The Princes of the blood stood behind the throne. In the whole assemblage, the royal Princesses alone were seated. After a brief interval, Their Majesties entered, and as soon as they had taken their places on the throne, the presentations were made. This done, Their Majesties rose and left the Throne Room, and the levee was at an end. It was midnight when I reached my hotel.

The next day I went with Hamidullah Khan to visit Queen Alexandra. We were met on our arrival by Colonel Dunlop Smith, and a Lord-in-Waiting who had spent many years in India, Within the palace we were received by two of Her Majesty's maids-of-honour, both of them ladies of high rank. I had just begun a conversation with one of these ladies when a side door leading to an adjoining apartment opened, and Queen Alexandra came in to the room. As I was not facing this door, I was unaware of her entry, and should have gone on with my conversation if Hamidullah, who at once recognized her, had not drawn my attention to her presence. I immediately rose, and advancing a few paces made my obeisance. Her Majesty shook hands with me, and, leading me to a sofa, took her seat beside me. She also invited Hamidullah Khan, who stood with Colonel Dunlop Smith behind my seat, to sit down ; but, out of respect for her, he remained standing. Her Majesty's first words to me were "I am sorry you did not come to England when Edward was alive." I replied "It is indeed a misfortune that I could not come in his life-time ; but this does not lessen my good fortune in being permitted to pay my respects to his gracious and benevolent Queen." Then, seeing that Her Majesty was sad, I tried to turn the conversation into a channel less likely to revive painful memories. But she continued to talk of her beloved and honoured husband, for whom, throughout the remainder of her life, she never ceased to grieve. For the loss of those we love leaves a wound which fortune's richest gifts are powerless to heal. We were all deeply affected by her sad words ; and it was with difficulty that I restrained my tears, and said, "Your Majesty, there is no one in the world to whom affliction does not come ; but time brings resignation to all. I have suffered the loss of my mother, my two daughters, and my husband." On this, the Queen regained her composure, and we talked for a while on general subjects. Presently she sent for her photograph, which she presented to me, saying that it was taken on the last occasion when she attended the opening of Parliament with the late King. At this moment her daughter, the Princess Victoria, came in, and the Queen said to her, "You are very late." A general conversation ensued. I told Her Majesty that I had written a book of memoirs which had been translated into English with the title "An Account of my Life," and another in which I had told the story of my pilgrimage to Mecca. I begged her permission to send her copies of both these books, and she replied that she would much like to have them, and that I might be quite sure she would read them. She then asked me and Hamidullah Khan to sign our names in her visitors book, and when we had done so she said "Why have you not brought your daughters-in-law to see me?" I replied that they were at Nauheim with my second son, who had been in ill health for some time past, and had gone to Nauheim for the sake of the climate and baths. I added that I was about to join my daughters-in-law at Nauheim; but that, after the Coronation, if it should be Her Majesty's pleasure, they should be presented to her. On my saying this, Colonel Dunlop Smith, who was standing by me, told Her Majesty that my daughters-in-law were not accustomed to go abroad, as I did, in a *burqa,* and that it was only my position as a ruler that enabled me to use greater freedom.

The Queen told me she had a great desire to go to India. "I should have gone with Edward,"

Queen Alexandra.

she said, "if so much had not been said of the difficulties of the journey. Look at my daughter-in-law. She has been twice to India, and is proposing to go again." I said that, when King Edward visited India, the discomforts of the journey were undoubtedly great, but that conditions had much improved since then, and it was now possible to travel in India with ease and comfort. Her Majesty said that there was no prospect of her going to India in the near future; but that some day she hoped to fulfil her desire. She then talked of other things, including the Coronation, in reference to which she said that she would not be in London during the festivities.

The hour was now growing late; but the Queen seemed unwilling that our conversation should come to an end, and continued to lead us from one interesting topic to another. At length, feeling that I had already taken up far too much of her time, and unwilling to tire her by further prolonging my visit, I rose and bade her goodbye.

The same afternoon I called on Lord and Lady Minto. It was very pleasant to meet them again, and we had a long and friendly talk which I much enjoyed. Lady Antrim was also there. She greeted me most affably and made special enquiries about the Bhopal Ladies' Club. I was disappointed not to see Lady Eileen Elliot, who had been unwell, and had left London for a change of air. In the evening I returned to Redhill.

In June I spent three weeks at the St. Ermine's Hotel. Both my sons were with me. On account of the approaching Coronation, which was to take place on the 22nd of the month, London was very crowded and very gay. No .one who witnessed the joy with which the English people looked forward to and prepared for this great event, could have any doubt as to His Majesty's immense popularity.

The Coronation ceremony was performed with much state in the ancient Abbey of Westminster. The Princes and Chiefs of India who had received invitations to be present had been requested to be at the Abbey by 7 a.m. I was accompanied by my two sons, and by the hour appointed we had taken the places reserved for us. The Princes and Crown Princes from other parts of Asia with their nobles, and the ambassadors of foreign Powers, arrived and took their places at the same time. When the whole vast congregation was at length assembled, the members of the royal family entered the Abbey. The Prince of Wales entered a few paces behind the others; Queen Mary came next; and last of all His Imperial Majesty the King.

I shall not attempt to describe the magnificence of the scene, or the complicated and splendid ritual of the Coronation service. Full and graphic accounts of this, and of all the other ceremonies and pageants connected with His Majesty's investiture, may be read in the journals and newspapers published at the time. On the termination of the service, the King and Queen, crowned, and arrayed in royal robes, left the Abbey, and drove in state to Buckingham Palace.

Purdah considerations prevented me from taking part in the Coronation procession, and from attending the luncheon given by the Lord Mayor at the Guildhall, both of which events took place the following day. My two sons, however, went to the luncheon. In the evening there was a garden-party at Buckingham Palace, which I attended wearing a *burqa*. More than seven thousand guests filled the beautiful grounds of the palace, and the spectacle was one of indescribable brilliancy. At this party the Indian princes who had come to England for the Coronation were presented to His Majesty. My two sons were amongst those who received this honour. On shaking hands with Colonel Obaidullah Khan, His Majesty said "I hope I shall soon see you again in India." I was presented first to His Majesty, and then to the royal Princes and Princesses. I had the privilege of conversing with Princess Victoria, and with the Duke and Duchess of Connaught, and, later in the afternoon, with Her Majesty Queen Mary. I also had quite a long conversation with the Prince of Wales. The Prince, who has most engaging manners, looked very happy. He talked to me about the palace garden, and said "We often have great fun here."

10

A few days later, the King presented medals to the Indian Chiefs, and officers of the Indian army, who had attended his Coronation. The presentations were made at Buckingham Palace, and this was the last occasion on which I had the honour of meeting His Majesty in England. At the hour appointed, Their Majesties entered the hall in which the Chiefs were assembled, and passed through it into an adjoining apartment, into which each Chief was then summoned separately with his suite. After receiving their medals, which His Majesty pinned to their breasts with his own hand, they withdrew to the outer hall. My two sons entered and received their medals with me. When all the Chiefs had been decorated, the King, attended by the Prince of Wales, the Duke of Connaught, Lord Roberts, Lord Kitchener, and other distinguished persons, proceeded to the courtyard of the palace, where the officers of the Indian army were assembled in military formation. Having passed through the lines, His Majesty entered a pavilion erected on a raised platform, and the officers then approached one by one, and received their medals. After the distribution, His Majesty made a short speech which was loudly cheered by the crowds that had gathered to witness the ceremony. As the weather was very inclement, my kind friend Lady Minto, who was one of the ladies of the court, found me a seat in the Queen's apartments, from which I had an excellent view of all that took place in the courtyard. Before leaving the palace, the principal guests were presented and took formal leave of Their Majesties. I was presented with my sons, and in acknowledging my salutation His Majesty again said "I hope soon to see you in India."

After attending this ceremony, I left St. Ermine's Hotel, and returned to Redhill. During my stay in London I visited the Bank of England, St. Thomas' Hospital, Madame Tussaud's exhibition of wax-works, Kew Gardens, and several of the London County Council's schools. I was also present at a meeting of the East India Association. I made the acquaintance of a large number of distinguished people, and had the pleasure of renewing many old friendships. At the various social and public functions which I attended I met many Indian ladies and gentlemen who were either resident in London or had come to England for the Coronation.

CHAPTER XV

ON THE CONTINENT, AND HOME AGAIN

On the 26th July, we left England for the Continent. We first spent a week at Geneva, and then went on to Constantinople, visiting Vienna and Budapest on our way. We reached Constantinople a few hours after crossing the Turkish frontier. In informing His Majesty the Sultan of my intended visit, I had requested that my arrival should be regarded as private. His Majesty, however, sent Raghib Bey, an officer of his court, to receive me on his behalf. I was also met by the Secretary of the British Ambassador. After a brief exchange of compliments, I drove, in company with Raghib Bey, to the Pera Palace Hotel, where accommodation for my party had been engaged.

On the third day of my visit, I called on the British Ambassador at Therapia. His Excellency very kindly sent his private launch for me, and received me on the steps of the landing-stage. He subsequently returned my visit, and was kind enough to arrange an audience for me with their Majesties, the Sultan and Sultana.

On the day appointed for the audience, Raghib

Bey came to the hotel, and conducted me and my two sons to the Dolma Baghchah palace. We were met at the entrance by a second court official, who led us up various flights of stairs, and through numerous corridors, into a magnificent reception room where tea and coffee were offered to us. After a short interval, a third courtier appeared, and we were ushered into another apartment where the Sultan awaited us. We made our salutations after the Turkish fashion, and my two sons kissed His Majesty's hand. After this, the Sultan, who had received us standing, invited us to sit down, and we all took our seats on chairs. We talked for a short while, and then the Sultan himself conducted me to the *harim* to visit the Sultana. Again I was led through innumerable corridors and galleries. At length we came to one where a guard of eunuchs was on duty, ranged in two long lines. Passing between them, we entered another apartment of a similar description, except that the eunuchs were replaced by female attendants, and from here the Sultan led me to a reception room within the *harim*. We had not to wait long before the Sultana, accompanied by one of her ladies, entered the apartment. I saluted them both, and we kissed hands in the Turkish fashion. The Sultana spoke in the Turkish language, and I in Persian, while the Sultan acted as interpreter between us. Presently His Majesty left us, saying as he did so "You will talk with more comfort if you remove your veil. I am going to take coffee with the British Ambassador and the Sahibzadas." After this I talked without my veil, and a daughter of one of His Majesty's secretaries came in to interpret. The Sultana's manner to me was kind and gracious. It had been a great pleasure to her, she said, to receive my visit. After the interview, Lutfi Bey, the Sultan's Chamberlain, showed us over the palace. We stayed eight days in Constantinople itself, and then moved to Therapia, a beautiful summer resort on the shores of the Bosphorus.

A peculiar interest always attaches to relics of the past. Amongst such objects none excite our veneration more than those connected with the origin and history of the faith we follow. Istamboul is one of the treasure-houses of Islam, and the foremost desire of every Mussalman who enters this city is to visit the Imperial *toshakhana*, and view the precious relics which are there preserved. Only the truly religious can have any idea of the spiritual comfort and joy which comes to those who make this pilgrimage. The objects comprising this sacred collection include a coat and footprints of the Holy Prophet, a manuscript copy of the Quran of Hazrat Usman, the swords of Umar, Abu Bakr, Usman, and Ali, and the holy banner under which the armies of Islam first marched to battle. We were unable to see the holy dress, as this priceless relic is kept under lock and seal, and is exposed to view only on one day in the year. On that day, the 15th of the blessed month of Ramazan, the Sultan himself breaks the seal, and exposes the dress to view. When it has been displayed, it is again locked up, and the Sultan affixes a new seal. I had, however, the happiness of seeing another garment which had belonged to the Holy Prophet, an undoubtedly genuine relic, which is in the custody of the descendants of Hazrat Owais-i-qurani. The copy of the Quran mentioned above was that which Hazrat Usman was reading at the time of his martyrdom ; the marks of his blood are still to be seen on it. In the *tosha-khana* we saw a man embroidering the cover for the holy Kaaba which every year the Khalifa sends to Mecca. As he worked he chanted verses from the Quran in a voice as sweet as David's. Before I left Constantinople, His Majesty made me unspeakably happy by bestowing on me a hair of the Holy Prophet. In return for such a gift, what had I to offer but my prayers ? His Majesty also gave me a cloth from the grave of the Prophet, and the historic mirror used by Sultan Mahmud I.

I had intended to spend the month of Ramazan in Constantinople, and then go on to Jerusalem ; but, learning that the season was unsuitable for visiting Palestine, I altered my arrangements, and, instead of remaining at Constantinople, went to Budapest. As the fast was already in progress, I found the journey very fatiguing, and decided to take a few days' rest before proceeding further. I met the British Ambassador here, and also the famous Professor Vambery. From Budapest we went to Venice, and thence to Florence, where we celebrated, or did our best to celebrate the *Id-ul-fitr*; for what *Id* could there be for us in a land where no mosque existed, and where the entire Moslem community consisted of our own tiny party?

At Florence I received a letter from Hakim Nur-ul-hasan informing me that plague had broken out in my State. This intelligence caused me much uneasiness, and, when other letters came telling of the seriousness of the outbreak, and of the suffering and distress which prevailed, I decided to return to Bhopal as speedily as possible, and gave orders that passages were to be booked on the first available steamer. At Brindisi, our port of embarkation, more letters reached me, confirming the previous reports.

The ship which awaited us at Brindisi was to take us as far as Egypt only. It was a very small boat, and I could not help thinking it would have great difficulty in weathering a storm. But we were in a hurry to proceed, and could not wait for another. We left Brindisi at six o'clock in the morning, and almost immediately encountered bad weather. The little steamer rolled about in a most disquieting manner, and, excepting myself, Hamidullah Khan, Munshi Liaqat Ali, and a maid-servant, every member of the party was very seasick. On reaching Port Said, we were placed in quarantine, because we had come from Venice where there was cholera. I found a cable from Nawab Nasrullah Khan awaiting me, which stated that the plague was raging in Bhopal, and that the daily death-rate in the city had reached 150. This made me all the more anxious to hurry on; but the steamer which was to take us to Bombay was not due for three or four days, so we had to wait as patiently as we could at Port Said. I cabled to Nawab Nasrullah Khan to move his residence to some uninfected locality, and to meet me on arrival at Bombay.

Finding I was compelled to make some stay at Port Said, I wired to Lord Kitchener, who had expressed his desire to see me, to say that I had reached Egypt, and proposed to pay him a visit. On receipt of my telegram, he notified my arrival to the Khedive, who, on learning that I was coming to Cairo, was kind enough to place his saloon carriage at my disposal for the journey, and ordered the Governor of the city to welcome me on his behalf. I accordingly travelled in the Khedivial saloon to Cairo, where I was received by the Governor and one of Lord Kitchener's Secretaries. A guard of military police was drawn up on the platform, and motor cars were in readiness to take me and my party to Shepherd's Hotel, where accommodation had been secured for us.

Besides visiting Lord Kitchener, I had, whilst at Cairo, the pleasure of meeting the Khedive's brother, Muhammad Ali Pasha, a man of much learning, and keenly interested in education. Want of time unfortunately prevented me from visiting the famous university of Azhar ; but I saw the mausoleum of Hazrat Imam Husain, in which the martyr's head is said to be buried, and I visited and offered prayers at the shrines of Hazrat Sakina, Hazrat Zainab, and Hazrat Nafisa. I was unable to see the Khedive, as he was not in Cairo. He wrote to me inquiring the probable length of my stay, and I replied that I was leaving Egypt almost immediately. For our return journey to Port Said, he again lent us his saloon, and provided us with dinner *en route*.

We left Port Said the following day, and, after an uneventful voyage, arrived safely at Bombay. I had been informed that the chief officials of the State were anxious to come to Bombay to meet me, and that preparations were being made at Bhopal to accord me a public reception. I was greatly touched by these proofs of the affection and loyalty of my people. But my heart was heavy with sorrow. I was coming back to a city of mourning, and I felt that I could not make my return the occasion for public rejoicings. I, therefore, intimated to the reception committee that it was my desire that my arrival should be private, and that no public demonstrations should take place. At my request only Nawab Nasrullah Khan, Maulavi Sayad Nasir-ud-din, the Revenue Minister, and Munshi Mansab Ali, the Financial

Secretary, came to meet me on landing. Nawab Nasrullah Khan wished me to remain for a time at Bombay; but this I declined to do. During the voyage, I had taken the precaution of getting all the members of my party inoculated against plague.

We reached Bhopal at 4 p.m. on the 23rd of October.

CHAPTER XVI

I ATTEND THE IMPERIAL DURBAR

In replying to an address of welcome presented to him on his arrival in India by the Bombay Municipality, Lord Hardinge read a cable he had that morning received from England, containing the announcement that His Majesty the King would hold an Imperial Durbar in India on the 1st of January, 1912. In a few hours these glad tidings were telegraphed all over India, and the whole country literally shouted with joy. Although this announcement was not official, the manner in which it was made by Lord Hardinge left no doubt in the minds of the people that they were at last to have the joyful privilege of welcoming to their midst their beloved Emperor and Empress, whom their eyes had never yet seen, but to whom in their hearts they paid unceasing homage.

A Royal Proclamation issued in London announced that the Durbar would take place on the 1st January, 1912. But, as this date coincided with the first of the month of Muharram, and as the first ten days of this month are observed by Muhammadans throughout the world as a period of mourning, His Majesty, out of consideration for the feelings of his Moslem subjects, was graciously pleased to alter the date of this great event to the 12th of December, 1911.

Invitations to attend the Durbar were issued to the ruling Chiefs by the Viceroy in the form of *kharitas*.[1] I was at this time in Europe, and the *kharita* containing my invitation was entrusted by the Political Agent to Nawab Nasrullah Khan, who forwarded it to me. Its contents were as follows:

MY ESTEEMED FRIEND,

I have it in command to communicate for the information of Your Highness a copy of the Royal Proclamation of the 23rd day of March, 1911, in which His Imperial Majesty King George V, Emperor of India, is graciously pleased to announce his royal intention to hold an Imperial Durbar at Delhi on the 12th day of December, 1911, for the purpose of making known in person to all the Princes and peoples of India the solemnity of his Coronation in London.

In compliance with the said command of His Majesty the King-Emperor, it is now my duty to invite your Highness to the Royal Presence at Delhi on that auspicious occasion.

I remain, with much consideration
Your Highness's sincere friend,
HARDINGE OF PENSHURST,
Viceroy and Governor-General of India.

(1) A *kharita* is a bag containing a letter to or from a person of distinction. The mouth of the bag, which is often elaborately embroidered, is tied with a silken cord, to which the sender's seal is attached.

To this *kharita*, which reached me at Redhill, I despatched the following reply:

MY ESTEEMED FRIEND,

I beg Your Excellency to accept my thanks for your *kharita* of the 29th April, enclosing a copy of the Proclamation in which His Majesty has graciously announced his intention to hold an Imperial Durbar at Delhi on the 12th December next. I am extremely grateful for the honour of being invited to the Royal Presence at Delhi on that auspicious occasion, and shall consider it my duty to attend. I am at present in England and am about to have the privilege of witnessing His Majesty's Coronation in London, and I rejoice that I am to have the additional privilege of paying homage to His Majesty at the forthcoming Imperial Durbar at Delhi, an occasion which is without parallel or precedent in the history of the Indian Empire.

I remain, with much consideration,
Your Excellency's sincere friend,
SULTAN JAHAN,
Ruler of Bhopal.

The Bhopal camp at Delhi was prepared by Maulavi Nasir-ud-din, under the supervision of Nawab Nasrullah Khan. Everything was done in accordance with the special instructions issued by the Government of India, and in consultation with the officers in charge of the durbar arrangements. The camp was tastefully laid out and decorated, while due regard was paid to economy. By the time I returned from my European tour, the preparations were well advanced, and the finishing touches were added under my own instructions.

The Bhopal Imperial Service troops were sent to

Delhi to take part in the grand review. My own body-guard was also sent, as well as a detachment of the Reserve Police Force to keep guard over the camp. The size of my retinue was within the limits prescribed by the Government of India. It was composed of members and relatives of my family, officers of the State, and the necessary complement of attendants and servants, most of whom were sent on in advance. On account of the outbreak of plague in Bhopal, I had, since my return from Europe, been living in camp at Sanchi, and it was from here that I set out for Delhi. I left by special train at 3-30 p.m. on the 30th November, taking with me the members of my family and a few chosen officers, including the Nasir-ul-muham and my Private Secretary. We reached Kingsway station at 10-30 the next morning. Representatives of the Government came to the station to receive me, and the customary salute was fired from the fort. A guard-of-honour was drawn up outside the station, and escorted me to the camp.

I devoted the next few days to sight-seeing and paying and receiving visits. On the 5th December, I attended a sectional meeting of the All-India Educational Conference, over which, at the request of the managing committee, I had consented to preside. The subject for discussion was female education. A large and magnificent pandal had been erected for the meetings of the conference, and on this occasion special accommodation had been arranged for purdah ladies. By 9 p-m., the hour at which the meeting commenced, every seat in the pandal was filled. I was received at the entrance by Nawab Viqar-ul-mulk and Sahibzada Aftab Ahmad Khan, and having been formally installed as president, I opened the proceedings by an address in which I dwelt on those aspects of the problem of female education which it seemed to me should engage the special attention of the conference. At the conclusion of my address, Shaikh Abdullah, the secretary of this section of the conference, read his annual report, after which the meeting was addressed by Mrs. Naidu, the well-known poetess and lecturer, and by Mrs. Sarala Devi Chaudhrani. Mrs. Naidu spoke with much earnestness and good sense, and her delivery was clear and persuasive. Mrs. Sarala Devi might have made a good speech had she been able to steer clear of national politics, her references to which were wholly out of place at a meeting of an essentially non-political character. The last speaker, Shams-ul-ulama Shibli, took for his subject "The women of Islam," on which he delivered a learned discourse full of allusions to the history and traditions of Islam, on which subjects he is a leading light. The proceedings terminated with a vote of thanks to me for presiding. This was proposed by Sahibzada Aftab Ahmad Khan. In response I said that, if the leaders of the Moslem community were induced by this meeting to take a more lively interest in female education, I should be more than rewarded for anything that I had been able to do. Before returning to my camp, I entered the screened portion of the pandal, and had an interesting talk with the ladies who were seated there.

This Conference has done much good work, and it is to be hoped that every educated Muhammadan will do his utmost to further its aims, and to establish it on a permanent basis. That such an organization has come into existence, and is meeting annually to confer on educational questions, is a welcome sign of national vitality. I pray Almighty God to bless its labours and make them fruitful.

Their Imperial Majesties entered Delhi in state on the 7th of December. Detailed instructions as to the order of their reception had been issued and distributed to all concerned, and two days beforehand the whole ceremony had been rehearsed. The ruling Chiefs assembled in the fort at 9 a.m., and awaited Their Majesties' arrival in a small but imposing pavilion erected near the Salimgarh station, and close to the magnificent *shamiana* in which the reception was to take place. The latter was of immense dimensions and exquisitely decorated within and without. On a raised dais in the centre were two golden chairs for the King and Queen, and in front of the dais was spread a scarlet carpet with a border of gold, on either side of which the princes who were to be presented ranged themselves in two bejewelled lines. The royal train arrived exactly at ten o'clock, and, as soon as the first ceremonial greetings had taken place, a royal procession was formed, and a few moments later, Their Majesties entered the *shamiana*, and, passing between the lines of saluting Princes, mounted the dais, and seated themselves in the golden chairs. The several Princes then passed in front of the dais from left to right, Sir Henry McMahon, the Master of the Ceremonies, calling out the name and titles of each as he approached. His Majesty was in the uniform of a Field-Marshal; he wore the Star of India, and carried in his hand a Field-Marshal's baton. The Queen's dress was of white satin exquisitely embroidered with flowers of the sacred lotus. This work had been designed and executed in India, and was a superb example of the Indian embroiderer's art.

The Chiefs, after passing before the dais, withdrew to the pavilion where they had originally assembled. When the last of them had been presented, Their Majesties descended from the dais and left the *shamiana*. Attended by the Viceroy and the Secretary of State, the King inspected the guard-of-honour drawn up at the entrance, and a procession was then formed to conduct the royal party to the camp. This time His Majesty was on horseback, while the Queen rode in a carriage of state. The Chiefs, splendidly arrayed and splendidly attended, joined the procession. On reaching the famous Ridge, from which, in the days of the mutiny the imperial forces bombarded Delhi, a halt was made whilst His Majesty received an address of welcome from the members of the Legislative Council. The address was read by Mr. Jenkins, who, at its conclusion, called for three cheers for Their Majesties, which were given with the utmost enthusiasm. In a loud and clear voice, which reached to the outskirts of his huge audience, the King thanked the members of the Council, and, through them, the people of India, for their warm and loyal greetings. His words were the signal for another great ovation; and the procession moved onward amidst a storm of cheers, which enveloped and kept pace with it till the royal camp was reached.

At 10-25 a.m. on December 8th, I had the honour of a private audience with His Majesty. My three sons, the Muin-ul-muham, and the Nasir-ul-muham accompanied me to the royal camp. I was met at the entrance by an Aide-de-Camp who conducted me to the Hall of Audience, where a guard-of-honour was drawn up. My sons and the two ministers awaited my return in another apartment. The Hall was divided by a curtain into two portions. The throne was in the second or innermost compartment, and it was here that the private audiences took place. Ordinarily the Chief who was to be received entered the first chamber with his attendant nobles. The curtain was then lifted, revealing the King seated on his throne. The Chief then advanced alone into the inner chamber, and the curtain was again lowered.

On entering the royal presence, I made my obeisance in the Bhopal fashion. His Majesty stood up to receive me, and graciously acknowledged my salutations, while an Aide-de-Camp placed a chair for me on the left side of the throne. Before taking my seat I expressed my devotion to His Majesty and my loyalty to the British throne. In doing so I said, "It is my constant prayer that Your Majesty may enjoy a long and happy life, and that the benign shadow of British rule may never cease to rest, like the shadow of the wings of Huma,[1] on the heads of the people of India. May Your Majesty visit this country again and again, and may your subjects long enjoy the blessings of your rule, and have the happiness of celebrating Your Majesty's silver, golden, and diamond jubilees". I made this little speech in Urdu, and the Foreign Secretary translated it into English. His Majesty appeared very pleased with what I had said, and thanked me for my good wishes.

Before taking leave, I read an address of welcome which I presented to His Majesty in a golden casket. This was a model of a boat, or State barge, being propelled by Indian rowers: in the windows of the cabin were photographs of

1 The Persian word *huma* signifies a bird of good omen, a Phœnix. It is supposed that the head overshadowed by the wings of the *huma* will one day wear a crown.—Ed.

myself and my children. In presenting it I said it was a humble offering to my sailor King. His Majesty examined the casket with interest, and said, "I greatly appreciate your gift." Sir Henry McMahon brought *attar* and *pan*, which the King offered to me with his own hand, after which I made my salam and withdrew.

The address which I presented on this occasion was as follows :—

"MAY IT PLEASE YOUR IMPERIAL MAJESTIES,

With one voice the peoples of India render thanks to the Almighty for vouchsafing to them the long-anticipated and inexpressible joy of welcoming to their midst their august Sovereign and his Imperial Consort. There is not one amongst them who does not feel that, to-day, his country is an earthly paradise.

The beloved name of Victoria the Good is a household word throughout the length and breadth of this land, where the blessings enjoyed during her long and happy reign will ever be thankfully remembered, and where we, who count ourselves her children, shall never cease to hold her name in honour. Nor will the name of her beloved son and successor, Edward the Peace-maker, be less reverently cherished for his unceasing solicitude for the well-being of his Indian subjects. But Your Majesties' claim to the gratitude of India is not only great, but unique ; for this is the first time in the history of British rule that her peoples have enjoyed the honour of being visited by their Sovereign and his Queen ; and we are one and all deeply beholden to Your Majesties for so graciously undertaking a journey of many thousands of miles to gratify the innate desire of your Indian subjects to render obeisance to the persons of their liege Lord and King, and the gracious Lady who shares his throne. It is, therefore, no matter for wonder that, at the coming of Your Majesty to celebrate his coronation in the ancient capital of India, the whole land resounds with shouts of joy. Your Majesty will, I hope, permit me, the only, and perhaps the last woman Ruler in this country, to raise my humble voice in unison with this happy chorus.

On the occasion when Your Majesty visited India as Prince of Wales, I had the proud distinction of being decorated by your own royal hands. In the long list of the Rulers of Bhopal, I am the only one to whom so great an honour has fallen. I am also the first to have had the privilege of witnessing the coronation of a British Sovereign in Westminster Abbey; and it is with unspeakable pleasure that I now take part in celebrating that happy event in my own country.

I beg Your Majesty to accept this address as a humble token of fidelity towards Your Imperial Majesty's person and throne, not only on behalf of myself, my family and my people, but of the entire Muhammadan community, and, I would add, of every other community in Your Majesty's Indian dominions. It would be impossible in this address to make adequate reference to the manifold benefits which this country enjoys under Your Majesty's rule; I would only assure Your Majesty that there is not a responsible or right-minded person in India to-day by whom these benefits are not recognised and appreciated with feelings of intense gratitude.

In conclusion, I join with my fellow Chiefs in proffering to Your Majesties my sincerest congratulations, and in wishing you a long, happy and glorious reign. May your glory endure as long as the sun and the moon endure in the heavens."

At twenty minutes past eleven the same morning, His Excellency Lord Hardinge paid the return visit on behalf of the King. All the ceremonial prescribed for such visits was carefully observed. Four Sardars of the State were sent to escort His Excellency to my camp. I awaited his arrival with the Political Agent at the entrance to the durbar *shamiana*. He came attended by his Foreign and Private Secretaries, an Under-Secretary, and four A.D.C.'s. As he descended from his carriage and entered the *shamiana* a British guard-of-honour, specially detailed for the occasion, presented arms, and the State band played a welcoming air.

His Excellency took his seat with me on a dais in the centre of the *shamiana*. The members of his staff sat on the right side of the dais, and the Political Agent and State officials on the left side. There was a formal conversation, after which the Political Agent presented the Sardars and officers, each of whom offered his *nazar*, which was touched and returned. The visit terminated in the customary manner with the distribution of *attar* and *pan*.

In the afternoon I went to see His Majesty lay the foundation stone of the All-India King Edward Memorial. A large open space close to the fort had been selected as the site of the memorial, and at 3 p.m. all the Chiefs assembled on this spot. A beautiful garden had been laid out, and in the centre, where the stone was to be placed, a handsomely adorned *chabutar*, or platform, had been erected, around which a regiment, of which his late Majesty had been Colonel-in-Chief, was drawn up in the form of a square. At 3-40 p.m. the King, accompanied by the Queen, arrived in an open carriage. They were received at the entrance to the garden by the Viceroy and the members of the memorial committee. The latter were presented to His Majesty, after which His Excellency read an address, and, on behalf of the Committee, requested His Majesty to lay the stone. The ceremony was then performed with all the customary rites. On its completion, the guns of the fort fired a salute, and Their Majesties returned to their camp.

On the morning of the 9th, Her Majesty the Queen received a deputation of Indian ladies, who presented an address to her, to which she was graciously pleased to reply through an interpreter. In the afternoon there were polo and football matches, at both of which Their Majesties were spectators. On the 11th, the King presented colours to various regiments. This ceremony took place on the polo ground, and was witnessed by immense crowds. The King arrived on horseback, and the Queen in a landau. Her Majesty watched the proceedings from the royal pavilion, where all the distinguished visitors then in Delhi were assembled. When the presentation of colours had taken place, His Majesty received the royal salute. He then inspected and addressed a few words to the Indian regiments which were present, after which he dismounted from his horse, and drove back with the Queen to the camp.

The 12th of December was the day reserved for the great durbar, the day to which the people of India had been so eagerly looking forward, and on which they now, and will ever look back as one of the brightest in their country's history. An elaborate programme of the proceedings, every feature of which had been planned and timed with the utmost exactitude, together with full instructions as to the ceremonial and etiquette to be observed, had been issued to those invited to witness, or take part in this splendid pageant.

By the hour appointed the nobles and ladies of the Imperial court, the ruling Chiefs, the great officers of State, the representatives of foreign Powers, and other persons of distinction, had assembled in the magnificent and densely-crowded amphitheatre. Each Chief was attended by the nobles and principal officers of his State. My retinue included my three sons, the Muin-ul-muham, the Nasir-ul-muham, and several other Sardars and officers.

When all had taken their places, His Excellency the Viceroy and Lady Hardinge, with the members of the viceregal staff, entered the amphitheatre, the whole assemblage rising and saluting. His Excellency's arrival was followed by the State entry of Their Majesties the King and Queen.

Their Majesties were attended each by six pages, the sons of Indian ruling Chiefs. My grandson Sahibzada Wahid-uz-zafar Khan was one of those in attendance on the King. My other grandson, Sahibzada Rafiqullah Khan had been chosen as one of the Queen's pages ; but it was thought that the weight of Her Majesty's train might be too much for him; so he was appointed instead to attend Her Excellency Lady Hardinge.

The King was crowned, and in his royal robes, and his breast was decorated with medals and orders. The Queen's robe was of white satin, and she was adorned with priceless jewels. Their Majesties were received by the Viceroy at the entrance to the central *shamiana*, and as soon as they had taken their seats on the dais, the Master of the Ceremonies in a loud voice declared the durbar open.

I do not propose to enter into a detailed account of this famous scene, every incident of which has been frequently and fully described by other writers. The royal speech followed the opening ceremony, after which the Viceroy, the Commander-in-Chief, the officers of State, and the ruling Chiefs in order of precedence, approached and paid homage to Their Majesties. I, too, made my loyal submission on this occasion. The Government had granted me permission to do so accompanied by a page, and Sahibzada Zulfiqar Muhammad Khan attended me in that capacity.

After receiving these tributes of allegiance, Their Majesties left the *shamiana*, and proceeded to the royal pavilion. The pages bore their trains, and they were followed at a short distance by the Viceroy and Lady Hardinge, Lord Crewe, Secretary of State for India, the Duke of Teck, the Mistress of the Robes, and other nobles and ladies of the court. On reaching the pavilion, they mounted and took their seats on the superb dais on which the royal chairs had been placed, and which was in full view of the vast concourse of people which had assembled on the mound.

Drums and bugles were now sounded, and in the silence which followed a Herald read the proclamation announcing the coronation of His Majesty on the 22nd day of the previous month of June. The same was then read in Urdu by the Deputy Herald, the Hon'ble Malik Umar Hayat Khan of Tiwana. Drums and bugles again sounded, and then the massed bands played the National Anthem, the troops presenting arms, and the whole audience standing. When the bands ceased playing, the troops fired a *feu-de-joie*, which was followed by a royal salute from the guns of the artillery.

After the salute, His Excellency the Viceroy ascended the steps of the dais, and, with courtly deference, received from the hands of the King the firman which it was His Majesty's pleasure should be announced on this occasion. His Excellency bowed profoundly, and, having descended from the dais, advanced to the front of the pavilion, and in a loud voice read the imperial order. When he had finished the bugles once more sounded, and the Herald called for three cheers for Their Majesties. The response was tremendous. Each time the Herald raised his hat in the air shouts of acclamation went up, not only from every side of the great arena, but from the troops without, and from the multitudes on the mound. Their Majesties were evidently deeply touched by this spontaneous outburst of loyalty, and repeatedly bowed their acknowledgments.

When the cheers at last subsided, the King returned to the *shamiana*, and, standing in front of the throne, made the historic announcement that the partition of Bengal had been annulled, and that from that time forward the city of Delhi was to be the capital of the Indian Empire. This was the final scene; and when the King had ceased speaking, the Master of the Ceremonies declared the Durbar at an end. The massed bands played a triumphal march, and the King and Queen, their faces radiant with smiles, took their seats in the State coach, and drove away amidst the renewed plaudits of the assembly.

CHAPTER XVII

AT DELHI AFTER THE DURBAR

On the 13th December Her Majesty received the Maharanis at the royal camp. I attended this reception with Birjis Jahan Begam. Excellent arrangements for purdah ladies had been made. As I was the Ruler of a State, Her Majesty talked to me first. She was very kind and gracious, and spoke of the previous occasions on which we had met in London. She next conversed with the Maharani of Baroda, and then with each of the others, showing to all alike the same royal courtesy. Before taking leave, I presented Her Majesty with an embroidered silk bag which I had worked myself.

At the same hour the officers of the Imperial Service Troops, and other Indian military officers, were received by the King. The Bhopal officers were presented by Colonel Obaidullah Khan. His Majesty was kind enough to enquire after the health of the Colonel Sahib, of whose indisposition he had been informed during our visit to London.

In the evening there was a grand garden-party

in the fort, which was attended by all the chiefs, and many other distinguished guests. Their Majesties arrived at 4 o'clock, attended by the Viceroy and the Secretary of State with their staffs. Their Majesties moved about freely, and talked with many of the guests, the chief of whom were afterwards presented in a room in the fort. The King had come to the party in civilian dress: but he presently exchanged this for the royal robes, and, with the crown upon his head, proceeded to the *darshan jharokha*, or "window of the appearance," overlooking the Jumna; and here, after the manner of the Mogul kings of former days, he showed himself to the common people, who, in expectation of this longed-for vision, had gathered in tens of thousands along the opposite bank of the river. I stood for a long time with the Maharani of Orcha and some other ladies watching the many-hued multitude, swarming not only over the banks but down into the parched bed of the holy stream, which seemed to have been transformed into a river of loyalty and happiness.

After leaving the *darshan jharokha*, the King received the ruling Chiefs, who were presented to him in the Rang Mahal. Nawab Nasrullah Khan and Sahibzada Hamidullah Khan were both present at this reception. When it was over, His Majesty said to Hamidullah Khan, "Is not your Mother here?" Hamidullah said that I was, and at once ran to find me. I was still watching the crowds on the river-bank when he came up and told me that the King had inquired for me. I hastened back with him, and was just in time to see Their Majesties before their departure. They received me very cordially, and, after a few kind words, shook hands with me, and bade me good-bye.

At 10 a.m. on December 14th, the King held a review of all the troops that were assembled at Delhi. After riding through the ranks, His Majesty took up his position at the saluting base, where the royal standard was hoisted, to witness the march past. The Queen attended the review in a carriage escorted by the Imperial Cadet Corps, and, having driven slowly past each regiment, joined the King at the saluting base. As soon as the march past had taken place, Their Majesties drove back to their camp. The Bhopal Victoria Lancers took part in this review. They were greeted with ringing cheers as each squadron galloped past in a perfectly-kept line. His Majesty declared himself much pleased with their performance, and recalled his previous inspection of the regiment at Indore, in 1905. I was unfortunately prevented from witnessing this review by the serious indisposition of Colonel Obaidullah Khan. In spite of his weakness, the result of nearly two years of continuous ill-health, he had fully made up his mind to be present, and to lead his regiment in the march past, and both General Beatson, the Inspector-General of Imperial

Service Troops, and his deputy, General Grimston, had been informed that he would do so. But the cold climate of Delhi had so aggravated his malady that Major Smith, his medical adviser, would not consent to his taking an active part in the review. He was, therefore, obliged, to his great and lasting disappointment, to announce his inability to lead his regiment on this great and unique occasion. His Majesty noticed his absence, and, on being informed of the cause, despatched his own physician to see him. At 1 p.m., accordingly, he came to my camp. "Their Majesties," he said, "have heard with much concern of your son's indisposition, and have sent me to you as, in a recent conversation with the Queen, you expressed a desire to take my opinion." I at once took him to see the patient, whom he examined with great care. When he had finished, he assured me that his complaint was not of an alarming nature. "The heart," he said, "has been strained, and is consequently in a weak state; but it will, I hope, soon become strong again. I will try to get you a new medicine which is now being used in cases of this nature. Unfortunately, it is not procurable in India, but I will get some of it from France and send it to you." Before departing he again spoke reassuringly of my son's condition. We thanked him most heartily for his advice and the trouble he had taken, and begged him to convey to Their Majesties our grateful appreciation of their sympathy and kindness.

At 9-30 in the evening, an investiture was held in the royal camp. In accordance with a pre-arranged programme, those who were title-holders, and those who were to be invested, reached the camp at 8-15, and entered the tents which had been pitched for them in front of the durbar *shamiana*. Each Chief came attended by his retinue, but only one or two of the latter were allowed to accompany him to his tent. No special formalities were observed during this part of the proceedings. I took with me my three sons, and entered my tent precisely at the hour appointed. When all had arrived, we went in procession to the *shamiana*. The Companions and Commanders of the various Orders led the way, followed by the Knights Commanders, the Knights Grand Commanders and Knights of the Grand Cross. I entered with the last group. Our seats were arranged in two lines on either side of the space in front of the royal dais. The *shamiana* had been very beautifully decorated. The roof was sky blue. The walls on either side were draped in a darker shade of the same colour. The hangings on the wall behind the dais were purple, and the dais itself, on which were two massive gilded chairs, was covered with a carpet of crimson and gold.

His Excellency the Viceroy with Lady Hardinge entered the *shamiana* shortly before 9-30. His Excellency was wearing the robe of a Grand Commander of the Star of India, with numerous other decorations. A few minutes later, a flourish of trumpets announced the arrival of the King and Queen. The band played the National Anthem as Their Majesties entered, and, hand in hand, proceeded to, and took their seats on, the dais. Lord Crewe, the Duchess of Devonshire, the Mistress of the Robes, and other members of the court followed in procession, and took up positions on the right and the left of the dais.

On this occasion Her Majesty the Queen was invested with the premier Indian Order. This was the first and most interesting feature of the proceedings. Rising from her seat, Her Majesty bowed to the King, and withdrew from the dais attended by the Viceroy. After a brief interval she again presented herself before His Majesty courtesying ceremoniously. The Viceroy approached at the same time, bearing on a velvet cushion the star and other emblems of the Order, other officers following with the robe. Her Majesty was then formally invested, the King himself pinning the star to her robe. At the conclusion of the ceremony the Queen, in accordance with an ancient and royal custom, kissed the King's cheek, and His Majesty returned the salute.

Other Orders and medals, which had been awarded on the 12th December, were next presented. The Maharani of Bhavnagar and I were invested with the Order of the Crown of India, and Her Excellency Lady Hardinge received the Kaisar-i-hind medal of the first class.

H. I. M. Queen Mary.

The Maharani wore her national costume, and was unveiled. The entire ceremony occupied more than two hours. Whilst it was in progress there was a fire alarm, which caused some uneasiness, but did not interrupt the proceedings. We learnt afterwards that a peon with a letter to deliver had left his bicycle, with the lamp burning, leaning against the tent of Lord Crewe's Private Secretary. The tent caught fire and was burnt down. Fortunately there was no wind, and the fire was extinguished before it could spread to other tents.

By making me a member of the Order of the Crown of India, His Majesty bestowed on me one of the most coveted of Indian honours. I take a special pride in belonging to this Order, because it was instituted by that great and illustrious Queen, Victoria the Good, for the purpose of conferring distinction on members of her own sex. Prior to its institution there was not, in the whole world, a single Order to which a woman could be elevated as a reward for merit ; though in every age there have been women, as well as men, who have done noble and courageous deeds, and devoted their lives to the good of others, or their country's service. Hence the title C. I. is valued not only because its possession is a high honour, but because it is a token of her late Majesty's affection for the women of India. Both my grandmother, the Nawab Qudsia Begam, and my mother, Nawab Shah Jahan Begam, received this title, and I am profoundly grateful to His Excellency for recommending me for the same distinction, and to His Imperial Majesty, King George V, for accepting the recommendation and conferring this great honour upon me. This was not the only favour shown to my family on the occasion of the Imperial Durbar. His Majesty was gracious enough to raise my eldest son, Nawab Nasrullah Khan, to the rank of Major in the British Army, and to make Colonel Obaidullah Khan a Companion of the Order of the Indian Empire.

On the 15th December, His Majesty laid the foundation-stone of the new city of Delhi. This historic function was witnessed by a large and distinguished gathering, which included the Ruling Chiefs, and representatives of all the provincial governments. Those to whom invitations had been issued reached the site at 9-30 a.m., and were received by the Home Secretary. Their Majesties arrived at 10 o'clock, and were received by the Viceroy and the members of the Executive Council. His Majesty was in the uniform of a Field-Marshal, and the Queen wore a gown of grey satin, ornamented with Kashmir embroidery in delicate shades of pink and mauve. The proceedings which followed were similar to those witnessed at the laying of the King Edward Memorial stone, except that on this occasion, when the King had completed his part of the ceremony, a second stone was laid by the Queen. When the rite had been thus doubly performed, the chief Herald, by royal command, made proclamation that the foundation-stone of the new city of Delhi, the future capital of India, had been laid by His Majesty the King-Emperor.

On the 16th December, Their Majesties left Delhi. At 10 a.m. the Chiefs attended a farewell reception in the durbar *shamiana*. An Aide-de-Camp received them and conducted them to their seats. These were arranged in order of precedence, the Chief of the highest rank being placed farthest from the throne, so that he might be the last to bid Their Majesties farewell. All wore their coronation medals, which had been distributed to them as they arrived at the *shamiana*. The proceedings were of the briefest and simplest description. Their Majesties entered the *shamiana* at 11 o'clock, and, having been received with the customary formalities and salutations, said good-bye to each Chief in turn, after which they passed out to their carriage and drove to the fort. A few minutes later the booming of guns told the people of Delhi that Their Imperial Majesties had left the city.

On December 18th, I left Delhi by special train, and reached Bhopal at six o'clock the same evening.

The services of two Bhopal officers were lent to the Government in connection with the royal tour. Sardar Abdul Aziz Pasha, who was Mir Bakshi, or Paymaster, of the Bhopal forces, and a pensioner of the British Government, was appointed *morchhal*[1] bearer to His Majesty; and Captain Amir Ahmad, an officer of the Imperial Service Troops, was placed in charge of the royal baggage train. Captain Amir Ahmad held the post of Secretary to Colonel Obaidullah Khan, who had a high opinion of his capabilities. The officers of the Government and of His Majesty's staff were completely satisfied with the manner in which he discharged the duties allotted to him, and he was given the title of M.V.O. in recognition of his valuable services.

After my return to Bhopal I received the following letter from General Drummond:

MY ESTEEMED FRIEND,

I take an early opportunity of informing Your Highness of the excellent work done by your Lancers at Delhi during the concentration for the Coronation Durbar. All ranks showed the greatest zeal and willingness in carrying out the various duties assigned to them. They presented a splendid appearance on the day of the Review, and marched past in a manner which called forth the admiration of military experts, and of the spectators in general. The King-Emperor's message to the army included the Imperial Service Troops, and His Majesty himself received your officers and expressed his admiration of their fine appearance.

May I congratulate Your Highness on the great success which has been attained in sending your troops to Delhi.

As I was unavoidably prevented from paying my respects to Their Majesties on Christmas Day and New Year's Day, I sent my loyal greetings

[1] A *morchhal* is a large fan made of peacocks' feathers, used for driving away flies.—Ed.

on both occasions by telegram. I give below copies of these messages and of the replies with which Their Majesties were gracious enough to favour me :

TO THE DUCHESS OF DEVONSHIRE,

Her Imperial Majesty's Camp, Ajmere.

Wish Your Grace most happy Christmas and shall be grateful if Your Grace will tell Queen-Empress that all my sons, myself and family send Her Imperial Majesty heartiest greetings of the season.—Sultan Jahan Begam of Bhopal.

TO THE PRIVATE SECRETARY TO HIS IMPERIAL MAJESTY,

King-Emperor's Camp.

My sons and pages of His Imperial Majesty together with all members of my family, and myself, wish a most happy and bright Christmas to His Imperial Majesty.—Sultan Jahan Begam of Bhopal.

TO THE PRIVATE SECRETARY TO HIS IMPERIAL MAJESTY,

Calcutta.

I shall be much obliged if you will kindly convey to Their Imperial Majesties my loyal and sincere wishes that the New Year, both Hijra and Christian, may bring all happiness and blessings to the King-Emperor and Queen-Empress.—Sultan Jahan Begam of Bhopal.

TO HER HIGHNESS SULTAN JAHAN BEGAM OF BHOPAL.

I am commanded by the Queen-Empress to thank you for telegram of Xmas-tide good wishes from Your Highness and sons. I also thank you for your kind message to myself.—Duchess of Devonshire.

TO HER HIGHNESS THE BEGAM OF BHOPAL.

I sincerely thank Your Highness, your sons my pages, and the members of your family for your kind wishes for Christmas, which I most heartily reciprocate.—George R. I.

TO SULTAN JAHAN BEGAM OF BHOPAL.

The Queen-Empress and I sincerely thank Your Highness for your kind greetings for the New Year, and we wish all possible happiness to you and prosperity to your State during 1912.—George R. I.

In Bhopal, on account of the havoc caused by the plague, the celebrations which took place on the day of the coronation durbar were of a very simple character. All thought of public festivities was abandoned on account of the sorrow and suffering which prevailed; for there was scarcely a household in which the disease had not claimed its victim. Moreover, many people had fled from the town, and this, combined with the absence at Delhi of the chief officials of the State, rendered demonstrations on a grand or extensive scale impossible. Still the day was observed, if not with great circumstance, yet in a spirit of true loyalty. The programme included a royal salute from the guns of the fort, the last gun being fired exactly at noon, the release of a number of prisoners from the State jail, and the feeding and distribution of clothes to seven thousand poor people. But the most impressive feature of the day were the services in the mosques, at which thousands of Mussalmans sent up prayers to the King of all Kings, who invests with sceptre and crown those whom He chooses to be His regents on earth, for the long life and prosperity of their beloved Sovereign and his Consort, and for the permanence of the British Empire.

On the 8th January, 1912, I went to Bombay to bid Their Majesties good-bye. I was accompanied by Nawab Nasrullah Khan, Colonel

Obaidullah Khan, the Revenue and Judicial Ministers, and Munshi Abdus Samad, my Military Secretary. On the morning of the 9th, I and my party had the honour of being received by His Majesty on the Apollo Bunder. His Majesty was kind enough to express pleasure at seeing me, and graciously accepted a bouquet of flowers which I presented as I took my leave.

CHAPTER XVIII

THE YEAR 1912

In March I went to Calcutta on a visit to Their Excellencies Lord and Lady Hardinge. I left Bhopal at seven o'clock in the morning, and reached my destination at three in the afternoon of the next day. I was met at the railway station by an A. D. C., who conducted me to Hastings House, which had been placed at my disposal, and where I stayed as Their Excellencies' guest. I lost no time in calling on my hosts. My visit was informal, as was also the return visit which His Excellency paid me at Hastings House.

On the occasion of my next visit to Viceregal Lodge, Lady Hardinge took me to a meeting of the Legislative Council, and on our return we discussed my scheme for a college for the higher education of women, and Her Excellency's scheme for a medical college for women. Both these institutions were to be founded in memory of Queen Mary's visit to India, and, as the need for each was equally urgent, we agreed to help each other in every possible way. Lady Hardinge afterwards sent me a copy of her scheme. As I read it through, I saw how great were the benefits which would result from the establishment of such a college as she had in view; and when I returned the scheme to her, I enclosed in my letter a donation of thirty thousand rupees.

I had several conversations with Lord Hardinge, in one of which he told me that he had commenced to learn Urdu, and asked me what books I advised him to read. I mentioned several, and, after my return to Bhopal, I sent him others which I thought would be of assistance to him. I met many European and Indian ladies in Calcutta, including Lady Creagh, the wife of His Excellency the Commander-in-Chief, Lady Jenkins, whose acquaintance I had made at Mussoorie, and the Rani of the late Prince Jagat Singh, who came to see me at Hastings House. Lady Jenkins gave an "At Home" to which she was kind enough to invite me. It was an excellently arranged and a most enjoyable party. Lady Jenkins was kind and attentive to everyone. She expressed great pleasure at meeting me again, and greeted me like an old friend.

The day before I left Calcutta, I received a deputation from the Islamia Orphanage. The children of the Orphanage came also. I was deeply touched as I looked on their innocent faces and thought of their homeless state. There is no doubt that by establishing this home the Mussalmans of Calcutta have rendered a great service to their community; for the children are not only fed and clothed, but are given sufficient training to enable them to earn their livings and lead useful lives. There are similar homes in other parts of India, but the demand for such institutions is still far in excess of the supply. In times of scarcity or pestilence, hundreds of Moslem children take refuge in orphanages established for other communities, where they are left without any instruction in their own religion. If the Muhammadans of India were to extend a larger charity to the fatherless and destitute, they would not only lay up for themselves treasure in heaven, but make it possible for many Moslem children to escape lives of poverty, misery, and sin, and grow up to be respectable, and perhaps honoured, members of their community.

I returned to Bhopal on March 10th, my visit to Calcutta having lasted just a week.

Throughout her Indian tour Queen Mary took the keenest interest in all that concerned the women of India. She came amongst them with an understanding mind and a heart full of sympathy, and her earnest solicitation for their welfare and happiness made a deep impression throughout the country, and gained for her the affection and gratitude of women of every class and creed,

It was my great desire that the whole of India should unite in raising a worthy memorial of Her Majesty's visit, and of her sympathy and affection for the Indian peoples. After my return from Delhi I turned over in my mind the various scheme that had occurred to me, and I came to the conclusion that no memorial would be more suitable, or more pleasing to Her Majesty, than an institution designed to advance the cause of female education, and I accordingly brought forward my proposal for the establishment of a college for the higher education of Indian women. I proposed that the college should be located at Delhi, the future metropolis of India, that it should be open to girls of every denomination, and that it should be named after Her most gracious Majesty, Queen Mary.

The first person to whom I disclosed my scheme was Lady Hardinge, who, as I have already said, gave it her hearty approval. She not only promised to assist me in every way she could, but assured me I might rely on the powerful support of His Excellency. I subsequently discussed the matter with several of my European friends, and also with the Chiefs of Central India, whom I met at a council meeting of the Daly College. I secured promises from the latter that they would explain my plans and views to their Maharanis, and Begams, to whom I should shortly be addressing my appeal for funds. In the meantime I had my scheme printed in pamphlet form both in English and Urdu. I also opened a subscription list which I headed with a donation of a lakh and twenty thousand rupees. The Qaisar Dulhan and the Shahriar Dulhan each promised to subscribe seven thousand rupees, and Shah Bano

Begam five thousand. The college was to be furnished and equipped with all the requirements of a thoroughly up-to-date educational institution; and the students' quarters were to be built and arranged in such a manner that the daughters of either wealthy or poor parents would be able to find accommodation suited to their means. I estimated that sixteen lakhs of rupees would be required to start the college, four lakhs for the building and its equipment, and eight lakhs to constitute an endowment fund.

My proposal was freely criticised in the press. It met with a certain amount of opposition; but there was a large balance of opinion in its favour. I wrote and published a pamphlet dealing with the main objections brought forward, and I wrote privately to certain Maharanis and others who had communicated their objections to me by letter. Throughout I remained in constant communication with Lady Hardinge, for whose assistance and encouragement at this time I can never be too grateful.

I had no reason to be dissatisfied with the result of my first appeal for funds. Her Highness the Dowager Maharani of Gwalior promised a donation of a lakh and a half of rupees. His Highness the Nizam of Hyderabad and Her Highness the Maharani of Gwalior promised Rs. 50,000 each, and His Highness the Maharaja of Jammu and Kashmir Rs. 10,000. Including the Bhopal donations, the total sum promised amounted to over four lakhs of rupees.

It is now, as I write, just a year since the publication of my scheme. The progress made has not been as great as I had hoped. Nevertheless, it has been steady; and I am confident that the funds required will be raised, and that in due time Queen Mary's College for Women will be established, and will take its place among the foremost educational institutions in India.

Amongst the administrative measures undertaken by me during this year, the most important was the foundation of a separate department for the management of the State police force, which up to this time had been under the control of the Judicial Department. I had long been desirous of carrying out this most necessary reform; but reasons, the nature of which I need not enter into, had hitherto rendered it essential that the police should be under the direct supervision of the Nasir-ul-muham; and had the separation taken place earlier, more harm than good would have resulted. As these reasons had now disappeared, and as the State police had, under the skilful management of Munshi Israr Hasan Khan, been transformed from an undisciplined levy into a regular and efficient force, I decided that the time for taking the desired step had arrived. In organizing the new department I had the assistance of Khan Bahadur Muhammad Sarwar Khan, an experienced police officer from the Central Provinces, whose services the Government were kind enough to place at my disposal.

In the month of November His Excellency Sir O'Moore Creagh and Lady Creagh accepted my invitation to visit Bhopal. The arrangements for their reception were similar to those made on the occasion of Lord Kitchener's visit. His Excellency inspected the fort and the military barracks, and witnessed a review of the State and Imperial Service troops. He expressed himself much pleased with all he saw, and spoke in very high terms of the work of Colonel Obaidullah Khan. I took Lady Creagh, who is keenly interested in female education, to see the Sultania and Victoria Girls Schools. A gymkhana was held on the parade ground in honour of His Excellency's visit, and in the evening there was a banquet at the Lal Kothi, but no speeches were made.

Colonel Obaidullah Khan had frequently spoken to me of the need for a military club in Bhopal; and as I approved of the idea, and had already granted a site for the club house, I requested Sir O'Moore Creagh to lay the foundation-stone, which he kindly consented to do. The ceremony took place on the 2nd November at 7 a.m., at which hour all the officers of the Bhopal army assembled on an elevated spot near the parade ground on which the building was to be erected. His Excellency arrived a few minutes later, accompanied by Lady Creagh, and attended by his staff. After formally welcoming them, I explained the circumstances which had led me to establish a military club in my capital. I briefly alluded to the benefits which the institution would confer on the officers of my army, and in their name I thanked His Excellency for the great honour he had done them in consenting to lay the foundation-stone. After performing the ceremony, His Excellency, in a short speech, emphasised the value of military clubs, and expressed the pleasure it had given him to inaugurate such an institution in Bhopal.

In the month of September I had received an invitation from the Hon'ble Mr. A. L. P. Tucker, then Agent to the Governor-General in Central India, to attend the opening of the new premises of the Daly College which was to be performed by His Excellency the Viceroy on the 8th November. I accepted the invitation with great pleasure and on the 7th November I left by the 10 p.m. train for Ujjain, where I arrived at six o'clock the next morning, and proceeded thence by motor car to Indore. As soon as I arrived I paid His Excellency a private visit, and afterwards attended the opening ceremony. The new college is a very handsome building. The large central hall, in which all the Chiefs of the Central India Agency assembled, had been beautifully decorated. When His Excellency arrived, Mr. Hyde, the Principal, read an address, giving a brief history of the college. In replying His Excellency expressed his pleasure at the increase in the number of the students and paid a high tribute to Colonel Daly, who had done so much to promote the welfare of the College.

He then reminded the Chiefs of the supreme necessity of giving their sons the best education possible, and urged them to see to it that their college lacked none of the means necessary for providing such an education. He expressed his regret that amongst the Chiefs who had been trained at the Daly College there were so few who took any important part in the administration of their States. Central India and Rajputana, he said, were greatly in need of enlightened administrators, and he earnestly hoped that every young Chief now being educated would, when he left the college, devote himself with energy to the duties and responsibilities of his position. Having brought his speech to an end with these wise and timely words, he formally opened the building.

After the ceremony, I went to a party given by Mr. Hyde. I met Lord Hardinge again at this function. I was talking to the little Nawab of Korwai, who was studying in the Daly College, as His Excellency came up to me, so I introduced the Nawab to him. Korwai is a small State in the Bhopal Agency. The Chief's family belongs to the same clan as my own, so we are consequently on very intimate terms. At the time of which I am writing, the Nawab was a lad of twelve. He is an orphan, and is being brought up under the guardianship of the Government.

CHAPTER XIX

LORD HARDINGE'S VISIT TO BHOPAL

If the reader will recall the momentous events of the year 1845, to which allusion is made in my banquet speech quoted at the end of this chapter, he will understand why it was that I attached a special significance to Lord Hardinge's visit to Bhopal. At the time to which I have referred, my grandmother, the famous Nawab Sikandar Begam, was Regent of Bhopal, to which position she had been appointed by the Government of Sir Henry Hardinge, afterwards Lord Hardinge, in recognition of her known talent for administration. Anxious that the Governor-General should see for himself the progress which the State had made under a woman's rule, she begged him to confer upon her the honour of being his hostess But those were not the days of easy and rapid travelling. The Governor-General found that the journey to and from Bhopal would occupy more time than he had at his disposal, and to the mutual regret of both parties, my grandmother's invitation had to be declined. It was a remarkable and happy coincidence that when 70 years later a similar invitation was sent, the granddaughter of Nawab Sikandar Begam was the ruler of Bhopal, and the grandson of the first Lord Hardinge was the Governor-General of India.

My invitation was sent in the form of a *kharita* in the month of July. His Excellency was kind enough to accept it, and expressed his desire that his visit should take place in the beginning of December. Preparations for his reception and entertainment were at once put in hand, and detailed instructions were issued to the departments and officers concerned. Everything possible was done to ensure the comfort of Their Excellencies, and of the numerous other guests who were invited to meet them.

To commemorate the occasion in a suitable and practical way, I decided to found two new institutions in Bhopal, a Military School, and an Infant Home, the former to be named after His Excellency, and the latter after Lady Hardinge. I also decided to ask His Excellency to open the Hamidia Library, which had been lately established and called after my youngest son Sahibzada Hamidullah Khan, and to ask Lady Hardinge to open the Lady Minto Nursing School to which I have referred in a previous chapter, and which had now been completed. Their Excellencies were consulted on all these points, and were pleased to accede to my requests. Such memorials as these bear permanent witness to our love and respect, while those who reap advantage from them will never cease to hold in honour the names of their benefactors.

Lord Hardinge of Penshurst

Their Excellencies were expected to reach Bhopal on the 4th of December, and by that date all our preparations were completed. The city was decorated as on the occasion of Lord Minto's visit, and the arrangements made at the Lal Kothi and the Guest House were on the same elaborate scale. At 9-30 on the day appointed I went to the railway station to receive my distinguished guests. My two elder sons, and the Revenue and Judicial Ministers accompanied me, while my third son took command of His Excellency's escort. A guard-of-honour was stationed on the platform, and the road from the station to the Lal Kothi was lined by the State Infantry. The Sardars and leading officials of the State, as well as my European guests, were assembled on the platform, where their seats were arranged in blocks. Amongst those present were the Raja Sahib of Rajgarh, and the Raja Sahib of Narsingarh.

The Viceregal train entered the station at 10 o'clock. I met His Excellency as he descended from his saloon, and was introduced by the Agent to the Governor-General for Central India, this being a necessary part of the formalities. Such of the Sardars as were entitled to an introduction were then presented by the Political Agent, and while this was taking place I met and welcomed Lady Hardinge, the formality of an introduction having again to be gone through. While the Sardars were being presented to Lady Hardinge,

I accompanied His Excellency in his inspection of the guard-of-honour. This completed the State reception, and we left the railway station in procession for the Lal Kothi, the Viceroy and myself leading the way in the first carriage.

Having conducted my guests to the Lal Kothi, I returned to the Sadar Manzil palace, from whence I sent a deputation, consisting of Colonel Obaidullah Khan, Munshi Israr Hasan Khan, Mian Tahsin Muhammad Khan, and Sardar Abdul Aziz Pasha, to make the customary *mizaj pursi*. The deputation was received by the Foreign Secretary, and, having made formal enquiry after the health of Their Excellencies, returned to the palace. At 11 a.m. I went to the Lal Kothi to pay my State visit. The Military Secretary, the Under-Secretary in the Foreign Department, and the First Assistant to the A.G.G., came to the Sadar Manzil to escort me to the Lal Kothi. Eleven Sardars accompanied me. On arrival I was conducted by an Aide-de-Camp to the durbar *shamiana*, which had been pitched on the lawn, and in which the interview was to take place. At the entrance to the *shamiana* I was received first by the Foreign Secretary, and then by the Viceroy, who stood one pace behind him. His Excellency led me to a chair on the right of his own. The Agent to the Governor-General, and members of the viceregal staff, sat on his left, whilst the Political Agent sat on my right, and next to him the State Sardars in order of rank. The proceedings were of the usual formal character. Each of the Sardars offered a *nazar* of one gold *mohur* to His Excellency, and those who were military officers, presented their swords to be touched. The visit concluded with the distribution of *attar* and *pan*. Before returning to the palace, I paid a formal visit to Lady Hardinge. Whilst this was taking place, His Excellency received the Rajas of Rajgarh and Narsingarh.

At 12-15 p.m., His Excellency paid the return visit. It is unnecessary for me to give an account of this function, as it took place in precisely the same manner, and was marked by the same formalities and ceremonial as the return visit paid to me by Lord Minto, which I have described in a previous chapter. At its conclusion, I sent Munshi Wahaj-ud-din and Munshi Maqbul Hussain Khan to wait upon Lady Hardinge, and bring her to the Sadar Manzil. Nawabzada Hamidullah Khan with Birjis Jahan Begam received Her Excellency as she alighted from her carriage, while I with my three daughters-in-law awaited her arrival in the palace. I introduced all my grandchildren to Her Excellency on this occasion, and I and my daughters-in-law presented her with specimens of our embroidery work. In the afternoon my European guests and the Sardars and State officers witnessed a gymkhana which had been arranged by Colonel Obaidullah Khan. The programme included various military sports and exercises, in which Nawabzada Hamidullah Khan was a successful competitor.

On the following day, December 5th, proceedings commenced with a visit to the Alexandra High School. An address of welcome was read by Munshi Anwarul Haqq, the Director of Public Instruction, and recitations in Urdu and English were given by the students, after which Lady Hardinge kindly presided at a distribution of prizes. From the school, a move was made to the Hamidia Library, which, as I have said above, His Excellency had consented to open. A gaily decorated *shamiana* had been erected in front of the library, and here a large company was assembled to witness the ceremony. In formally requesting His Excellency to open the building, I said:

"YOUR EXCELLENCY, LADIES AND GENTLEMEN,

I had not been many days on the *gaddi* of Bhopal before I realised the immense and urgent necessity of promoting the cause of education amongst my subjects, and especially amongst those of my own sex; for I knew that no scheme, however elaborate, for raising the standard of social life in Bhopal, could ever achieve its object if it failed to take into account the question of female education. While, therefore, I have endeavoured to provide for the youths of Bhopal the means of obtaining a sound and thoroughly up-to-date education, I have done all in my power to advance the training of girls and young women, and to make the institutions I have founded for that purpose as popular and as efficient as possible. The success which has so far been achieved gives me good ground for hope that my efforts will, with God's blessing, lead to still better results in the years to come.

It is a fact, which none can gainsay, that the British Government has infused new life and a new spirit into the educational activities of this country, and has thus laid the foundations of a new Imperial city of enlightenment and culture. Your Excellency, India will never forget that your renowned grandfather was among the first who sowed the seeds of education in this land, and we are, therefore, encouraged to hope that progress in the cause for which he did so much will be a prominent feature of your own term of office.

In the carrying out of my educational schemes, I have derived no little assistance from the examples set to the boys of the State by my youngest son, Sahibzada Hamidullah Khan, who, instead of going to a Chiefs' College, or being educated privately, joined the Alexandra High School, attending it regularly like an ordinary student. This led the nobles and leading families of the State to take a new and favourable view of modern education, while my son's studious habits and good manners had an excellent influence on his fellow pupils.

Ladies and Gentlemen, having created in my subjects a thirst for knowledge, it is only right that I should furnish them with the means of satisfying that thirst, and it is with this end in view that I have founded the institution which His Excellency is about to open. The Hamidia Library will contain both western and oriental works, and will cater for readers of all classes, young and old. There will also be a public reading-room supplied with newspapers, magazines, and other current literature. I have named the library after my youngest son because his example has done so much to forward my educational schemes. That it is to be opened by His Excellency will go far to ensure its success, and I am most grateful to him for consenting to perform the ceremony."

In reply to my speech His Excellency said :

"YOUR HIGHNESS,

I am very much touched by the reference you have made

to the work done by my grandfather in India in the cause of education, when its blessings were but little appreciated. His example has inspired me with the desire to follow worthily in his footsteps, and among the manifold cares which occupy my attention, there is none that is nearer my heart than the desire that, during my tenure of office, the basis of primary education may be so widened that elementary knowledge may gradually become the birth-right of the poorest in the land. At the same time it is my earnest hope that the profession of schoolmaster may become one of the most honoured of all, and that the whole tone of the teaching given, may be raised, so that its true end and object may, with greater certainty, be accomplished, and the generations of young men, who year by year go forth into the world and hold, each in turn, the honour and welfare of India in their hands, may ever be more and more fit, not only to maintain but to raise the tradition of the various professions and occupations, and while exhibiting a constantly increasing efficiency in the various walks of life, may bear testimony to the value of their early training by the steady development of individual character.

Your Highness has very truly remarked that an educational policy to be successful must include female education. You have doubtless realised that the principal difficulty in its development lies in the conservatism of the people themselves, which varies in strength, from province to province and from district to district, in its reluctance to allow the girls of India to participate in that enlightened instruction, which, I am glad to say, is slowly but surely passing over the land. There is no question that this reluctance is gradually being overcome, but the progress is slow, and I can only hope that the stimulus of Your Highness's energetic example may accelerate the speed, and that another generation will see almost as many girls at school as boys. It may seem a little curious that, in coming to open a library, I should have talked so little of books, and so much of education. But after all the association is fairly intimate, and those who reach the highest rungs in the ladder of education would find their powers of progress crippled and their faculties starved if they had no access to the learning gathered by the wise men of their own and other countries; while culture would be a poor thing if it did not stimulate that interest in all that is going on in the greater world, which it is part of the object of this library to foster and satisfy.

I have been much interested to hear of Nawabzada Hamidullah Khan's educational career, and I most cordially congratulate Your Highness upon the breadth of mind and wisdom by which you have been guided in this matter. I trust that his example may give an impetus to the cause of learning in Bhopal which may never loose its force, and I feel that it is a very happy inspiration which has led you to give his name to this institution. I have very great pleasure in declaring this Library open. I name it the Hamidia Library, and I wish it a most happy and useful career."

The building was then opened, after which His Excellency and all those present entered and inspected the library.

In the afternoon, Lady Hardinge and several other members of the viceregal party paid a visit to Sanchi. They were met on arrival by the Muin-ul-muham and the Nasir-ul-muham, who took them to see the famous Buddhist topes. Tea was served in the Sanchi State rest-house, and the party returned to Bhopal at 6 p.m. Lord Hardinge spent the afternoon at Sehore, where he played golf, and took tea with the Political Agent.

At 10 a.m. on December 6th, I took Lady Hardinge to the Sultania and Victoria Girls' Schools. At each institution the Lady Superintendent presented an address, and recitations were given by the students. At the Sultania School Her Excellency distributed prizes to a number of students. We next paid a visit to the Ladies' Club. Her Excellency first met the members in the central hall of the Club, and then went into another room, where the game of "Fishponds" was being played. On this occasion, the members of the Club collected amongst themselves the sum of Rs. 1,378 which they presented to Her Excellency as a contribution to the fund she was raising to assist the Turkish widows and orphans. This was in addition to the sum previously raised by the members at a former meeting of the Club. I had myself already contributed Rs. 9,000 to this fund ; and further sums of Rs. 1,500 each were now contributed by Qaisar Dulhan, Shahriar Dulhan, and Shah Bano Begam.

In the afternoon Their Excellencies and all my other guests watched a polo match between the viceregal staff and Bhopal. Nawabzada Hamidullah Khan played for Bhopal. The game was very interesting and exciting, and was won by the home team. In the evening a State banquet took place at the Rahat Manzil palace. The city and the road from the Lal Kothi to Ahmedabad were illuminated as on the occasion of Lord Minto's visit. I joined the party at the end of the dinner, with my three sons and the Revenue and Judicial Ministers. After the royal toast had been honoured, I proposed the health of Their

Ladies' Club, Bhopal.

Excellencies. My speech was as follows:

"YOUR EXCELLENCIES, LADIES AND GENTLEMEN,

With the deepest feelings of loyalty to our beloved King-Emperor, I rise to offer to his distinguished representative in India, to Lady Hardinge, and to all my other guests a most hearty welcome to Bhopal.

Your Excellency, amongst the civilized nations of the world, tradition, whether of race or family, has always been respected; but amongst us Orientals it has a peculiar value and significance, and we pay special honour to him who, in addition to his personal qualities, inherits the prestige of an ancient and historic name. We are all aware of the long and honourable association of Your Excellency's family with the British Crown, and of the notable services which your ancestors have rendered to the Empire in times of stress and difficulty. In India to-day there are few names better known or more highly honoured than that of Your Excellency's grandfather, the first Lord Hardinge. We have read in our childhood of his gallant deeds in England's wars in Europe, and how he was presented with Napoleon's sword; and afterwards when he became Governor-General of these dominions, we know how brilliantly he fulfilled the high expectations entertained of him by the Court of Directors of the East India Company. Those were troublous times for India, Your Excellency; but by his wise and fearless rule, Lord Hardinge restored law and order throughout the country, and opened the way to good government, peace and prosperity.

There is a remarkable resemblance between the career of that great soldier-statesman and that of his distinguished grandson, whose services won for him the high regard of Queen Victoria and of our late Emperor, and who has now been sent to represent his Sovereign in this country. Your Excellency, you have not been long amongst us, but you have already inspired us with confidence, and we look forward to a period of prosperity and progress under Your Excellency's administration.

Your Excellency, on the death of my grandfather, Nawab Jahangir Muhammad Khan, in 1844, it was Lord Hardinge who recognised the installation of my mother, Nawab Shah Jahan Begam on the *gaddi* of Bhopal. My mother was then but seven years of age, and Lord Hardinge sanctioned the appointment of Mian Faujdar Muhammad Khan (an uncle of my grandmother Nawab Sikandar Begam) as Regent of the State, enjoining him to devote himself to the duties of his office, and especially to the liquidation of the State debts. Lord Hardinge's *kharita*, which is in Persian, and is still preserved amongst the archives of the State, is a striking illustration of his solicitude for the welfare of my family and the people of Bhopal. Shortly after Mian Faujdar Muhammad Khan's appointment, serious dissensions arose, and Nawab Sikandar Begam, dissatisfied with the way in which the administration was being conducted, pressed her own claims to the Regency, which were eventually regarded with favour by Lord Hardinge's government. Nawab Sikandar Begam was duly installed as Regent of Bhopal in 1847, and with the happiest results. For the Sikandar Begam was an admirable administrator, and she not only introduced many salutary reforms, the benefits of which we are still reaping to-day, but succeeded in paying off the heavy debts which had so long stood in the way of progressive government. At the same time, by her services during the Mutiny, she amply demonstrated her faithfulness and devotion to the British Crown. Your Excellency, I cannot but feel very happy and proud that I, who am the grand-daughter and successor of the Nawab Sikandar Begam, have the privilege of entertaining the grandson and successor of the renowned Governor-General who recognised her regency.

I will not detain you, Ladies and Gentlemen, with a description of the various measures of reform on which I have been engaged during the past year. These are adequately dealt with in the annual Administration Report. I would like to say, however, that the new Settlement continues to work most satisfactorily, and has greatly facilitated the work of the Revenue Department. Signs of increasing prosperity are visible throughout the State. The revenue demand is now met willingly and regularly, and there is no accumulation of arrears, as was invariably the case under the old system. I have every hope that at the end of the next financial year, the State revenue will show a substantial advance.

As Your Excellency is aware, I spent a considerable part of last year in Europe, and my experiences in the various countries I visited have proved very useful to me. During my absence, the administration of the State was in charge of Nawab Nasrullah Khan, and it gives me great pleasure to say that he proved himself fully equal to his important position, the duties of which he discharged with great credit. I am very grateful to Your Excellency for recommending him for the rank of honorary Captain in the British Army, a distinction which will, I have no doubt, lead to his increased interest in military matters. My second son. Colonel Obaidullah Khan, has continued to render me valuable service as Commander-in-Chief in Bhopal. Nearly three-fourths of my army now consists of Imperial Service Troops ; but owing to the wise and economical management of Colonel Obaidullah Khan, the expenditure incurred by the Military Department is actually less than it was during my mother's rule, when the State army consisted largely of irregular troops. My youngest son is at present a student at the Aligarh College. I have excellent reports of his progress, and I am confident that he will grow up to be a credit to his family, and that he will rise to distinction in the service of the State and of the King-Emperor.

Almost exactly three years ago, Lord Minto, speaking in this banqueting hall, remarked that I was probably the only lady-ruler in the world who had seen active service. During my pilgrimage to Hedjaz, I certainly experienced some of the realities of war; and I assure Your Excellency that, should the emergency arise, not only will my entire army, horse, foot, and transport, be ready to take the field, but every member of my family, and I personally, will consider it an honour to place our services at the disposal of the King-Emperor and his Government. Nor would the participation of women in actual warfare be a new phenomenon in the history of my State. In the year 1812, the women of Bhopal not only defended their city against the repeated onslaughts of an investing force, but held it successfully till reinforcements arrived.

Ladies and Gentlemen, I crave your pardon for having trespassed so long upon your patience. I have now but one duty to perform, and that is the extremely pleasant one of asking you to drink to the health of my illustrious guests. Their Excellencies Lord and Lady Hardinge."

When the toast had been drunk, Lord Hardinge replied as follows :

YOUR HIGHNESS, LADIES AND GENTLEMEN,

"Your Highness has alluded in flattering and friendly terms to the old connection between the family of the Ruler of Bhopal and my own grandfather, and I most heartily reciprocate the feelings of good-will to which Your Highness has given expression, and it adds immensely to the pleasure of my visit here to know that we are now, in the third generation, renewing an ancestral friendship. My grandfather had the good fortune to be the Governor-General of India when the famous Sikandar Begam became Regent in 1847 ; and when I read the history of those times, I feel that there can have been few incidents in his tenure of office that he could look back upon with greater satisfaction than the part assigned to him in that event.

The Bhopal State under Your Highness's rule has maintained and excelled its previous record of loyalty to the British Crown, and I take leave here to remark that the earnest devotion to the Throne of the leading Mussalman Houses of India going forth to meet, as it does, His Imperial

Majesty's affectionate solicitude for his Muhammadan subjects, must be to the King-Emperor a source of the liveliest satisfaction.

In the case of Bhopal, friendly relations date from 1778, in which year the British forces marching from Bengal to Bombay received valuable assistance from this State. In 1813 the connection with the British Power was renewed, and in 1817 a treaty of alliance was concluded against the Pindaris. The works of Malcolm are evidence of the spirit in which that treaty was regarded by the then Ruler of the State. He says that "no obligations were ever more faithfully fulfilled." In the dark days of the Mutiny, which occurred during the rule of Sikandar Begam, no Chief in the length and breadth of India proved a more staunch ally than Her Highness. She kept the peace throughout her own territories, although the Maulvis in the city were preaching *jihad,* and her troops were threatening her life. The Agent to the Governor-General at Indore, Colonel Durand, and many others were given refuge and safety. Supplies and troops were sent to the assistance of the British as far north as Kalpi. The Begam sent a force to quell the revolted troops of the Bhopal contingent at Sehore, and saved the government treasury there. In recognition of these services, Queen Victoria conferred on Her Highness the title of G.C.S.I., and granted her the *pargana* of Barasia, which now forms part of the State. And if Her Highness was a faithful friend to the British Crown, she was no less a benefactress to her own State and people. She liquidated the State debts, reformed the judiciary, the police, and the mint, she abolished the pernicious system of revenue farming and trade monopoly, and showed her solicitude for the welfare of her poorer subjects by personal tours of inspection and enquiry into their condition. I think it must have been a source of keen satisfaction to my grandfather that he had seen Sikandar Begam's elevation to power in Bhopal. It is a source of equal gratification to me that the descendant of

Sikandar Begam, whom it is my privilege to meet now in Her Highness's beautiful capital, has carried even further her schemes for the amelioration of the condition of her subjects.

Your Highness is the proud possessor of the titles G.C.I.E. and G.C.S.I., and the King-Emperor himself conferred upon you the decoration of the Imperial Order of the Crown of India at Delhi last year. These are tokens of the King-Emperor's regard for Your Highness and of his recognition of your work as an administrator. Your Highness's sons, Sahibzadas Nasrullah Khan and Obaidullah Khan, have proved themselves your able coadjutors, and their services have been rewarded by the conferment of the rank of Major in His Majesty's Indian Army; and on the King-Emperor's birthday this year I was glad to announce that Sahibzada Obaidullah Khan was made a Companion of the most exalted Order of the Star of India. Your Imperial Service Troops are evidence of the readiness of the Bhopal State to take its part in the defence of the Empire. Lord Kitchener spoke most favourably of their efficiency and I have no doubt the addition to their numbers, gratefully accepted by His Majesty's Government last year, will maintain the same high standard. It was, I know, a source of disappointment to Your Highness that the Government of India were unable some years ago to utilise their services in the expedition against the Zakka Khel; but I am sure, should the opportunity occur in the future, they will acquit themselves most worthily.

In the matter of internal administration Your Highness's State is as well known as it is for its fidelity to the Crown. Your Highness has devoted to the good of your State and people the results of the wide knowledge acquired in England and by travel in many countries of Europe and Asia. to the extent of which the interesting book which Your Highness has recently published is a speaking testimony. I need not recapitulate the steps that have been taken in recent years to improve the administration, but I must mention two matters of special importance in which Your Highness set a brilliant example. I refer to the measures you have taken for the improvement of the lot of women, and the interest you have taken in the important question of the higher education of Chiefs and nobles. It seems almost to be forgotten sometimes that women are the mothers of men, so little has been done for them in some parts of India. The frightful infant mortality that prevails in the land, and the lack of education amongst women of all classes are matters of universal knowledge on which I need not expatiate. But they are none the less of the most paramount importance in the lives of all the peoples of India. The difficulties that lie in the way of improvement are immense; but Your Highness, as a woman who is also a Ruler, has opportunities which perhaps are given to no-one else. That Your Highness has made splendid use of them is shown by the work done in the Lady Lansdowne Hospital, the Madrassa-i-Sultania, and the Victoria Girls' School. Your Highness's pamphlet on the subject of the education of the Rulers and nobility of India shows that Your Highness has given deep consideration to this important subject, and it has done much to stimulate the movement. It is a matter in which I feel the greatest personal interest, and to which I am ready to give all the support in my power.

I need detain you no longer; but I must express my gratitude to Your Highness for the heartiness of your welcome to Lady Hardinge and myself, and for this extremely instructive visit to your wonderful State. Ladies and Gentlemen, I have great pleasure in proposing the health of that enlightened and loyal Chief and generous hostess, Her Highness the Nawab Begam of Bhopal."

When the speeches were finished, the guests ascended to a drawing-room on the first floor of the palace, where the Viceroy presented Nawab

Nasrullah Khan with a commission as Major in the British Army, and decorated Colonel Obaidullah Khan and Munshi Israr Hasan Khan respectively with the orders of the Star of India and of the Indian Empire. A display of fireworks, which the guests watched from a balcony, brought the evening's entertainment to an end. Unfortunately, some of the fireworks had been damaged by a shower of rain, which fell whilst they were being set in position ; so the display was not altogether a success.

On Saturday, the 7th, His Excellency witnessed a review of the Imperial Service and State troops. All the guests and the Sardars and officials of the State were present. Nawab Nasrullah Khan, in his new capacity as Major, was in attendance on His Excellency, and Colonel Obaidullah Khan, who was Commander-in-Chief of the Bhopal Army, took command of the troops, while Nawabzada Hamidullah Khan, who had lately been made an honorary Major in the State army, acted as his staff officer. After the march past, His Excellency, in a short speech, expressed his appreciation of the manner in which the various movements had been executed, and congratulated Colonel Obaidullah Khan on the efficiency of the forces under his command.

As soon as the review was over, the Viceroy, with Lady Hardinge and the Agent to the Governor-General, accoinpanied me to the site which had been selected for the Hardinge Military School.

A large gathering of military officers, Sardars and others was assembled on the spot, which was a small hill close to the parade-ground. In requesting His Excellency to lay the foundation-stone of the school, I said:

"YOUR EXCELLENCY,

This school, the foundation-stone of which you are about to lay, will, I have little doubt, do much to promote the efficiency of my army. I entirely agree with Colonel Obaidullah Khan, my Commander-in-Chief, in thinking that the fact of Your Excellency's laying the foundation-stone will impart a special significance to the school, and will be a source of pride and encouragement to the officers who receive their training within its walls.

The association of Your Excellency's name with this institution will also serve to perpetuate the remembrance of the good-will and friendship which your distinguished grandfather, that famous soldier and statesman the first Lord Hardinge, extended to the Bhopal State and its then ruler Nawab Sikandar Begam. The establishment of such an institution in Bhopal will, I am sure, be as pleasing to Your Excellency as it is to me, since it is to further the well-being of an army that inherits traditions of constant and unflinching loyalty to British Crown, an army that is as ready to-day, as it has ever been in the past, to fight for the honour of our beloved Sovereign and the safety of his dominions."

In reply His Excellency said:

"YOUR HIGHNESS,

Though I am not a soldier myself, there is a very strong military tradition in my family. My grandfather earned a distinguished name on the field of battle, and I have a son in the army who, I hope, may follow in his great-grandfather's footsteps; while my position in relation to the Indian army demands my constant attention to military questions. Most gladly, therefore, do I accept the task you have proposed for me.

I understand that the object which Your Highness has in view is to provide, firstly, an honourable career for the cadets of noble families in Bhopal, and, secondly, to secure that your troops—of whom you have so much reason to be proud—should be officered, and efficiently officered, by the flower of your own subjects. The scheme is one deserving of every support and sympathy, and under the eye of Your Highness and Colonel Obaidullah Khan I feel sure that it will prove a great success. The most important point in connection with it is that the instructors and resident masters should themselves be men of honourable record and good breeding such as can furnish not only teachers of the military art, but of all that a brave and chivalrous soldier and gentleman should be. A military career is by no means all glory and glitter; the glitter comes through sustained hard work and monotonous drudgery, and glory, if it passes by a soldier's way, can seldom be won unless difficult lessons of self-reliance, self-control, discipline, and courage have been thoroughly learned before the crisis comes.

In laying this foundation-stone, I am very proud to think that this school will bear my grandfather's and my name; and, while I hope that it will prove the greatest possible success for the purpose for which it is intended, I have also little doubt that it will be a very happy home and training ground for many brave young soldiers in the years to come."

The stone was then duly laid, after which His Excellency returned to the Lal Kothi, while I took Lady Hardinge and my other lady guests to the Lansdowne Hospital. Her Excellency inspected the hospital and then formally opened the Lady Minto Nursing School. We then went to the site selected for the Lady Hardinge Infants' Home, of which Her Excellency was to lay the foundation-stone. In asking her to perform this ceremony, I congratulated her on the rapid progress of her scheme for the establishment of a Zenana Medical College, by the initiation of which she was so worthily carrying on the great work for Indian women which had been commenced by Lady Dufferin and continued with such splendid results by Lady Lansdowne, Lady Elgin, Lady Curzon, and Lady Minto. Bhopal, I said, already possessed permanent memorials of two of these benefactresses in the Lady Lansdowne Hospital, established in my mother's reign, and the Lady Minto Nursing School, founded by myself; and it was because I desired that Her Excellency's name should be similarly preserved in my State that I had asked her permission to call the institution she was about to inaugurate, the Lady Hardinge Infant's Home.

Before laying the stone Lady Hardinge said:

"YOUR HIGHNESS,

You have mentioned the names of those in whose footsteps I follow, from Lady Dufferin onward, and I cannot tell you how great a privilege it is to me to be able to do my small part in the work so worthily begun by them. In pursuit of their ideals, it was some little time before I was able to decide in what channel my efforts could best be directed. But the support which the Zenana Medical College has received has given me assurance that amongst the many suggestions laid before me, there is none that meets more fully the immediate needs of India and India's women. I should like to take this opportunity of saying that alone I should have been quite helpless, and of thanking my many kind friends, which I do from my heart, for their sympathy and support, and for having made the scheme possible by their generosity. For not only is it possible, but I hope and think that its success is assured. To Your Highness I owe a debt of gratitude that cannot be paid for your great generosity and your kind co-operation. When I say that the success of the College is assured, I hope no one will think that further contributions will be unwelcome. The more we get, the greater will be our power for good and the wider our field for work, and it is a field that is practically limitless in extent.

As regards this proposed Home for infants, it needs no words of mine to extol its objects or justify its creation. I hope it may in the future be a very happy home for many little ones, and I feel that Your Highness has paid me a very high compliment in asking me to give it my name."

At 4 p.m. I gave a garden-party at Ahmedabad, which was attended by all my European and Indian guests. Shooting matches and outdoor games had been arranged for the entertainment of the company, and the party was a very enjoyable one.

At 6-30 the same evening Their Excellencies left Bhopal. I accompanied them to the railway station, where I bade them good-bye. Their departure was private.

As soon as I heard of the dastardly attempt made on the life of Lord Hardinge, and of the serious nature of His Excellency's injuries, I determined to go myself to Delhi and inquire after his welfare. Besides being the representative of His Majesty the King-Emperor, Lord Hardinge was an old and honoured friend of my family; and I felt that at such a time the least I could do was to express personally to him and to Lady Hardinge

Lady Hardinge.

my sympathy and condolences. I accordingly left Bhopal by special train on January 26th, and arrived the same evening at Delhi. My two elder sons accompanied me, and Sahibzada Hamidullah Khan came from Aligarh and joined us. We stayed in a camp that had been pitched for us in the grounds of Viceregal Lodge.

On the morning of the 27th, I paid a formal call at Viceregal Lodge. An Aide-de-Camp came to escort me from my camp, and His Excellency, with his customary thoughtfulness, sent a rickshaw for me; but, as the distance was very short, I preferred to walk. I was shown first into Lady Hardinge's private room. Her Excellency received me with great cordiality, and, before taking me to see Lord Hardinge, gave me a vivid account of the recent outrage, and told me of the anxiety she had since suffered on her husband's account. It was natural that she should tell me of all that she had been through; for, when perils and trouble are fresh in the mind, there is always comfort in speaking of them to a sympathetic listener. The courage which Lady Hardinge displayed during the terrible ordeal to which she was subjected, excited universal admiration, and will ever remain a splendid example to her sex.

At the end of our conversation Lady Hardinge took me and my three sons to see His Excellency, who received us with great kindness. In spite of the painful operations he had undergone, he appeared to be in good health, though his arm was still in a sling, and he was unable to shake hands with us. After the usual compliments, he led me to a sofa and took his seat beside me. I was anxious that my visit should not trouble or tire him , so, as soon as I had made inquiries after his health, and offered my congratulations on his recovery, I rose to take leave. Before we withdrew, my sons also offered their congratulations. Sahibzada Hamidullah Khan, who was the last to do so, expressed his sympathy with His Excellency, first on his own account, and then on behalf of the students of the Aligarh College, who, he said, were overjoyed to hear of His Excellency's recovery. Lord Hardinge thanked him for his kind words, and bade him assure his fellow students at Aligarh that he greatly appreciated their sympathy. Following an old Indian custom, I sprinkled their Excellencies with gold and silver flowers as I bade them good-bye. I also handed to Lady Hardinge an envelope containing notes to the value of Rs. 5,000, requesting her to devote this sum to charitable purposes, in whatever way she thought best.

On the same afternoon, His Excellency attended a meeting of the Imperial Legislative Council, the first to be held since the attempt on his life. The speech which he delivered on this occasion, and which the whole of India had been anxiously awaiting, deserves to be written in letters of gold. I shall make only one brief extract from it :

"I desire," he said, "to assure the whole of

India that my policy will be in no way affected by this occurrence. I shall continue the policy which I have followed during the past two years, without swerving from it by a hair's breadth."

This noble and magnanimous pledge, which he so amply fulfilled, gained for Lord Hardinge the undying respect of the people of this country. That so noble a Viceroy was made the victim of a murderous assault, and that the perpetrator of this disgraceful outrage was allowed to make good his escape, are circumstances which no Indian worthy the name will ever recall without feelings of shame.

CHAPTER XX

OTHER EVENTS OF THE YEARS 1911-12

IN this and the following chapter I shall briefly record sundry events of local interest which took place during the tenth and eleventh years of my reign.

On the 22nd June, 1911, the State celebrated the coronation of His Majesty the King-Emperor. The chief event of the day was a grand durbar which took place shortly before noon at the Sadar Manzil palace. As I was in England at this time, the durbar was presided over by Nawab Nasrullah Khan, who, in an eloquent speech, gave expression to the loyalty of Bhopal to the British throne, and to the feelings of affection and devotion with which Their Majesties were regarded by all sections of the people. At noon, a royal salute was fired from the fort, and food and clothing were distributed to the poor of the city. In the afternoon there were sports, in which the students of the various schools took part, and in the evening the Nawab Sahib gave an "At Home" which was attended by the principal officers of the State, and many other guests.

An important feature of this year was the census.

This was carried out in Bhopal in accordance with instructions received from the Indore Agency. The report issued on the completion of the work showed that the total population of the State was 738,124, being an increase of 72,208 since the census of the year 1901. Through the carelessness, or ignorance, of the census officers, the language spoken in the villages of Bhopal was described in the report as "Malwi". Why they went out of their way to invent this word I do not know. The language spoken throughout the State of Bhopal is Urdu, and, I may add, a purer form of Urdu than is to be heard in the villages of the Province in which that language originated.

By the grace of God, Bhopal escaped the fodder famine which this year prevailed in Ahmedabad, Gujarat, and the Bombay Presidency. Throughout the period of scarcity, the State had an abundant supply of fodder, and local dealers were able to export a considerable quantity to the stricken areas. As a humanitarian measure, I reduced by one-half the customs duty on all fodder exported to these districts.

A cotton mill had been set up in Bhopal in my mother's reign; but it had never been in charge of an expert, nor had it been managed on sound business lines. It had, in consequence, never proved a profitable concern. I had long been turning over in my mind what steps I should take in regard to this mill, and finally, on the suggestion of the Muin-nl-muham, I leased it to Sir Ibrahim

Rahmatulla, who was the owner of several other cotton mills, and a man of large business experience. Moreover, I felt confident that, as a co-religionist Sir Ibrahim would do all he could to promote the trade, and encourage the industries of an Islamic State; and on this account, and because of his high reputation as a financier, I was glad to have business connections with him.

At the commencement of my reign I established a full court of justice to assist me in deciding cases of appeal. It now seemed to me that this court could be dispensed with, and I accordingly abolished it. At the same time I ruled that all appeals, and cases for revision, were to go before the Secretaries of the Departments concerned and this is the procedure at present followed. After a full inquiry, all the papers relating to each case, together with the Secretary's report, are submitted to me, and I deliver judgment.

After the establishment of the nineteen years' settlement, many of the difficulties previously experienced in collecting the land revenue disappeared. There were still, however, a certain number of *mustajirs* who were invariably behindhand in their payments. I therefore made a regulation that, in future, all such defaulters should pay a fine amounting to five per cent. of their liabilities. In the following year, a marked decrease in the number of defaulters showed that the new regulation was having the desired effect. I gave orders that the money realized from these fines should be funded separately, and disbursed in the form of *taqavi* grants for the improvement of agriculture. Thus the fines levied from the foolish *mustajir* were used to benefit his wiser neighbour.

The tender plant of education, which I had raised from seed, and on which I had bestowed so much care, was now a sturdy sapling, and gave every promise of growing into a goodly tree. In the year 1911, the Alexandra High School sent up fifteen candidates for the matriculation examination, of whom ten were successful. In most cases those who matriculate proceed to one of the universities, or to some technical institution, to continue their studies. The State is always willing to give assistance in the shape of grants or scholarships to poor and deserving students.

It had been my intention to adopt in the Sultania School the course of study which was being prepared for the girls' school at Aligarh; but as time went on, and this scheme did not make its appearance, I grew tired of waiting for it, and I introduced the course prescribed for girls by the University of Allahabad. A number of girls reading in the Sultania School have already reached the middle class.

I have already referred to the outbreak of plague which took place in Bhopal during my trip to Europe, and in consequence of which I abandoned my plans for visiting Jerusalem and other places of interest. I mention the circumstance again because I wish to record my appreciation of the courage and devotion displayed by Nawab Nasrullah Khan in his efforts to alleviate the misery of my people. Throughout this trying period he remained in the city, regardless of his own safety, and left no stone unturned to provide aid for the sick, and to prevent the disease from spreading to other parts of the State.

In spite of his continuous ill-health, Colonel Obaidullah Khan continued to devote himself with unflagging energy and enthusiasm to his duties as Commander-in-Chief of the Bhopal army. During these two years special attention was given to physical drill, gunnery, and pioneer work, and officers were sent to Allahabad, Ambala, and other places, for training in these and other military duties. In 1911, the Imperial Service Troops reached full strength both in officers and men; and in the same year the State Infantry was reorganized, and renamed the Sultania Infantry, and was reserved, like the Victoria Lancers, for the service of the King-Emperor.

From the day when he assumed charge of the Military Department, it had always been the endeavour of Colonel Obaidullah Khan to revive in the people of Bhopal the martial spirit of their ancestors, and to induce them to join the State army. It was on his suggestion that the State undertook to provide those who enlisted with horse and uniform, the cost of which had previously to be borne by the recruit himself. But in spite of this and other concessions, many refused to take service on the ground that it was derogatory to their dignity to serve as ordinary sepoys or sowars. So anxious was the Colonel Sahib to make military service popular, that, to overcome this objection, foolish and reasonless though it was, he allowed as many as possible to join as officers. I only hope these men will prove themselves worthy of their responsible positions.

It was on the suggestion of Colonel Obaidullah Khan that a branch of the St. John's Ambulance Association was at this time established in Bhopal. All the officers of the army, and many of the leading citizens, became members of the branch, and ambulance classes were opened in the schools of the city, at the Central Hospital, and at all the village dispensaries. The State granted a substantial sum towards the maintenance of these classes, and I trust that ere long persons capable of rendering first aid to the sick or injured will be found in every village of the State.

I have now to record, with deep regret, the deaths of the following members of my family: Mian Yasin Muhammad Khan, Mian Aqil Muhammad Khan, Mian Yar Muhammad Khan, Mian Hamid Muhammad Khan, and Sardarbi Sahiba. Mian Yasin Muhammad Khan was the leading *jagirdar* of the State. He was one of the few members of his class who realized the value of education, and was himself an educated man. He was kind-hearted and philanthropic, and will be

15

remembered for his many charitable works. Mian Yar Muhammad Khan and Mian Hamid Muhammad Khan were Sardars of the old school. The latter was still a young man when he died. Though he had received no regular education, he took a lively interest in current affairs, and being a man of ability and intelligence, had acquired a position of considerable influence. He too will be remembered for his charitable deeds. Mian Aqil Muhammad Khan, an old-fashioned but high-minded gentleman, was the son of the step-brother of Nawab Jahangir Muhammad Khan, who was ruler of Bhopal from 1837 to 1844. On account of his near relationship, *jagirs* were conferred on him both by my grandmother and my mother. Sardarbi Begam was my mother-in-law. She was a very refined lady, and renowned for her piety.

The claims of the descendants of these deceased *jagirdars* were duly recognized by the State, and either lands or stipends were granted to them. I may here mention that amongst the *jagirdars* there are some who contract marriages with women who have no connection with their class. This practice is much to be deprecated, for the children of such marriages are nearly always neglected, and grow up without any kind of training. They are in consequence a credit to nobody, and as their fathers are not well enough off to make provision for them, their maintenance becomes a charge on the State.

In the year 1912, death deprived me of the services of three very able and valued officers. Khan Bahadur Maulavi Nasir-ud-din, C.I.E., was the victim of cholera, and Bakhshi Muhammad Hasan and Syad Nur-ul-hasan died of paralysis. Maulavi Nasir-ud-din belonged to a well-known Patna family, several members of which had risen to honourable positions under the Imperial Government. When his services were first lent to me he was holding the post of Junior Secretary to the Board of Revenue in Bengal. He came to Bhopal to take up temporarily the duties of Nasir-ul-muham. At the termination of this acting appointment, he returned to Bengal; but, as I had been much pleased with his work, and knew him to be an experienced revenue officer, it was not long before I again asked for the loan of his services. This time I appointed him to the office of Muin-ul-muham, rendered vacant by the retirement of Maulavi Nizam-ud-din Hasan, and he continued to serve me in this capacity until his death. The State owes much to his energy and ability. It was under his guidance that the nineteen years' settlement was brought into successful operation. The punctual payment of the land tax by the *mustajirs* of the State, who had been accustomed to look upon it as almost an hereditary right to be three or four years in arrears, was a sufficient proof of the efficiency of his administration. Though a strict officer, he always had in view the good of the people. He was in consequence both liked and respected, and his death was deeply regretted by all classes. I chose as his successor Maulavi Muhammad Ahmad, M.A., LL.B., Junior Secretary to the Board of Revenue in the United Provinces. This officer took charge in November, 1912. I trust he will fulfil the high hopes which his reputation and experience have led me to entertain of him.

Bakhshi Muhammad Hasan was over 80 years of age when he died. He came originally from Thana Bhavan, in the district of Saharanpur, but had long made his home in Bhopal. He was first brought to the State by my grandmother, Nawab Sikandar Begam, who took him into her service whilst at Mecca in 1863. He was a skilled accountant; and it was in that capacity that he has usually employed. He was the respected servant of three successive Begams of Bhopal. His manners were quiet and unassuming, and his honesty and faithfulness were a splendid example to all about him.

Hakim Syad Nur-ul-hasan received his medical training under the late Haziq-ul-mulk Hakim Abdul Majid Khan. He was physician of my *deorhi* when I was heir-apparent, and after my accession, on the death of Hakim Farzand Ali Sahib, I appointed him Afsar-ul-atbar, or State physician. Besides being skilled in the treatment of diseases of all kinds, he was of an exceedingly gentle disposition, and overflowing with sympathy for those who were sick or in trouble.

After being made State physician he refused to take any fees from his patients ; indeed, his whole life was dedicated to the service of humanity. During the plague epidemic, he visited the sick at all hours of the day and night, allowing himself no fixed time for food or rest, and taking few precautions for his own safety. His own son died of plague, and his younger brother also took the infection. Though he himself entered hundreds of infected houses, he never actually contracted the disease ; but his devoted labours, combined with grief at the loss of his son, told seriously on his health, and soon after the outbreak had subsided he became dangerously ill. As no medicines gave him relief, he went to Delhi for treatment. His condition, however, grew steadily worse, and in the month of Ramazan he was attacked by paralysis, and three months later he died. Thus passed away a very noble soul. Of Hakim Nur-ul-hasan it may be truly said that he lived and laid down his life for his fellowmen.

CHAPTER XXI

THE SAME CONTINUED

THE following distinguished persons visited Bhopal in the years 1911 and 1912 :—

(1) During my absence in Europe, His Excellency the Viceroy twice passed through Bhopal whilst on tour. On both occasions he made a short halt, and took tea with my son Nawab Nasrullah Khan.

(2) In March 1911, I had the pleasure of entertaining His Honour Sir John Hewett, Lieut.-Governor of the United Provinces, who will always be remembered for his magnificent staging of the Imperial Durbar, and for his successful organization of the first industrial exhibition ever held in India. I received much kindness and attention from Sir John Hewett both at Delhi and at Allahabad, and I was, therefore, specially glad of the opportunity of showing him hospitality. His visit was of a purely private character, and was mainly devoted to shooting in the Bhopal jungles.

(3) On the 28th February, 1912, His Highness the Maharaja of Kapurthala paid a visit to Bhopal. He was accompanied by the Maharani Sahiba,

who is a Spanish lady, his daughter Kunwari Sahiba, and a small staff. They spent the night in their saloon at the railway station, and in the morning, accompanied by the Muin-ul-muham, they drove through the city and visited various places of interest, including the King Edward Museum. In the afternoon they took tea with me at the Rahat Manzil, and in the evening I entertained them at a State banquet. Their Highnesses left Bhopal the same night.

(4) The heir-apparent of the Bhor State visited Bhopal and Sanchi on the 2nd January, 1912. He stayed in the guest-house in the Hayat Afza garden, and before leaving called on me at the Rahat Manzil. He appeared to be a dignified and refined young man.

(5) His Highness the Maharaja of Gwalior, accompanied by Sahibzada Sultan Khan, his Judicial Minister, and several State officers, came to Bhopal on the evening of March 18th. The Nasir-ul-muham and Mian Iqbal Muhammad Khan received him at the railway station, and conducted him to the Rahat Manzil, where I had prepared a banquet in his honour, which was attended by my two elder sons, and some of the principal Sardars of the State. I had made arrangements for him to remain for the night at the Rahat Manzil; but, as he was obliged to depart by the train which left Bhopal at 2 a.m., he preferred to sleep in his saloon at the station.

The Maharaja of Gwalior is an old friend of

mine. He treats me with as much respect as if I were his mother ; and the Dowager Maharani always calls me her sister. It is, therefore, always a pleasure to me to receive His Highness at Bhopal, and the more so because he is a prince of exceptional intelligence and ability. Under his energetic and enlightened rule there has been marked progress in every branch of the Gwalior administration. There are many Indian chiefs who would do well to take His Highness as their example.

(6) The Hon'ble Mr. Tucker, who was officiating as Agent to the Governor-General of Central India, in the place of the Hon'ble Mr. O'Dwyer, paid a semi-official visit to Bhopal in August. He was accompanied by Mrs. Tucker, and after a stay of two days left for Gwalior.

(7) On August 11th, Lord Sydenham passed through Bhopal on his way to visit the Buddhist topes at Sanchi. I went to the railway station to see him, and the Nasir-ul-muham and Captain Amir Ahmad were sent to Sanchi to make arrangements for his accommodation in the State rest-house. I knew Lord Sydenham very well, having frequently had the pleasure of meeting him in Bombay, on which occasions he had shown me much kindness and courtesy.

(8) A few days later, I had the pleasure of welcoming to Bhopal Sir Henry McMahon, who was then Chief Secretary to the Government of India in the Foreign Department. In the course of his two days' visit he saw all the sights of the

city, and spent some pleasant hours boating on the lake. I gave a garden party in his honour, and also a dinner, which was attended by my three sons, and the Revenue and Judicial Ministers. Sir Henry McMahon is a very distinguished political officer, with a wide knowledge of Eastern races and Eastern questions. He was placed on special duty with the Amir of Afghanistan when His Majesty visited India, and on that occasion rendered the Government very valuable service. By Muhammadans his name will be remembered with special honour, for they felt that he knew and understood them, and that they could always turn to him as a friend.

(9) My other visitors during these two years included the Hon. A. C. Brodrick, Mrs. Herbert Smith, Viscount Frankfort, Miss de Mont, and the heir-apparent of the Trikamgarh State.

In the year 1912 I was asked by Mrs. Porter to become the patroness of two clubs for Indian ladies which she had organized, one at Allahabad and the other at Lahore. I have always strongly advocated the establishment of such institutions as tending to raise the social status of women, and to advance the cause of female education. Accordingly, though I knew very little of the state of Indian society either in Allahabad or Lucknow, I wrote to Mrs. Porter and said that it would give me great pleasure to accede to her request. I congratulated her, at the same time, on the excellent work she was doing, and promised an annual donation to the funds of each club.

I also received a request from the Trustees of the Hostel for Muhammadan students at Aligarh that I would contribute towards the expenses of that institution, which, owing to lack of funds, was still in an unfinished state. I knew this institution was in low water, having heard a good deal about it from Maulavi Abdul Ghafur, Superintendent of the Bhopal Legislative Department, who had formerly been Superintendent of the hostel; and as the Maulavi had often spoken to me of the benefit which the students derived from being decently lodged and provided for, I felt that the Trustees were appealing for a worthy cause. I therefore sent them a substantial donation, and my son Sahibzada Hamidullah Khan did the same.

I consider that Muhammadans act more wisely by taking advantage of the existing Government schools and colleges, than by establishing Moslem Schools which cannot offer the same educational opportunities. But if this course is to be followed with advantage, hostels for Muhammadan students are essential; and these it is clearly the duty of the well-to-do members of the Moslem community to provide and maintain. The Aligarh trustees asked my permission to call the dining-hall of their hostel, after me, the Sultan Jahan Manzil. But to this I did not consent. The custom of associating the names of founders and benefactors with the institutions they help to bring into existence, has much to commend it; but I have never liked it in my own case. For it seems to me that if we are convinced that a particular cause, or institution, is in need of, and worthy of, our support, the rendering of such assistance as lies in our power becomes a religious duty; and a religious duty should be performed, not for our own glory, but for the glory of God.

About this time I read and heard much about the sufferings of the Turkish soldiers, and the miserable condition of the women and children left destitute by the Balkan war. I was much distressed by these accounts, and in the month of November I sent a donation of Rs. 21,000 to the Osmanli Red Crescent Fund at Constantinople. At the same time I opened a relief fund in Bhopal, and published an appeal for contributions in the State Gazette. In a little over a month 30,000 rupees were collected, of which 3,000 were raised by the members of the Ladies' Club.

Another committee was formed at the end of this year by Colonel Obaidullah Khan to collect money for the Moslem University. An appeal explaining the urgent need for this University was issued, and met with a most satisfactory response nearly all the principal citizens of Bhopal contributing according to their means. In this instance, too, the Ladies' Club was to the fore. It is a great gratification to me to know that my subjects are beginning to realize the needs of their community, and to take an interest in public movements; but what specially pleased me in connection with these two appeals was the practical support they met with from the ladies of the town. The interest and active participation of purdah ladies in such matters affords a striking proof of the progress that is taking place in the social life of Bhopal. Only those who know what the conditions of life in the zenana were at the commencement of my reign can appreciate the nature and extent of the change that a few years have wrought. Female education alone has made this progress possible; for without it the Princess of Wales Club, which has borne such excellent fruit, and all my other schemes for the betterment of the women of my State, would have been worthless.

Another appeal to which I could not turn a deaf ear reached me from Shams-ul-ulama Maulana Shibli, a man deeply versed in the history of Islam, who had untertaken to compile in Urdu an authoritative biography of the holy Prophet, and who was now asking for assistance to enable him to get his work completed and published. Up to this time there was not to be found in the whole of Urdu literature a single book containing a full and trustworthy account of the founder of our faith, and it seemed to me that it would be a grave reflection on the Mussalmans of India if the Maulana's labours had to be relinquished for lack of pecuniary aid. Accordingly, as soon as I had read his appeal, I wrote to him urging him to complete his compilation as soon as possible, and promising to send him the whole sum he asked for in his appeal. As this sum did not include the cost of the numerous works of reference which it was necessary for him to consult, my son Hamidullah Khan, being anxious to share the honour of helping forward so pious a work, sent him a further sum of Rs. 2,000, and promised to add to it should it prove insufficient. Colonel Obaidullah Khan was no less interested in the Maulana's task, and undertook, when the book was completed, to have it translated into English and published at his own cost. I rejoiced to see in my two dear sons these proofs of religious fervour; I am confident that, like true Mussalmans, they will never be backward in the service of their faith.

CHAPTER XXII

AN HONOUR'S LIST

BEFORE bringing this third volume of my memoirs to a close, it is fitting that I should record my appreciation of the services rendered to me by my three sons, and by the ministers and other officers of the State.

My eldest son, Nawab Nasrullah Khan, in addition to performing with ability the various important duties that have from time to time been entrusted to him, has twice acted as regent during my absence from Bhopal. On both occasions he proved himself a wise and capable administrator, and conducted the affairs of the State to my entire satisfaction.

General Obaidullah Khan, who had always displayed a keen interest in military matters, was made Colonel of the Imperial Service Lancers in 1904, and the following year was appointed Commander-in-Chief of the forces of the State with charge of the Army Department. In my speech at the Durbar held on the occasion of my last birthday, I referred to his services as follows: "I need not remind you of the many and beneficial reforms which Nawabzada Muhammad Obaidullah

Khan has introduced into the State Army. His management of the Military Department has shown us how efficiency can be combined with economy, and how all difficulties can be overcome by hard work and perseverance. His appointment is one entailing much mental and physical strain, and though, as you know, his services have been entirely voluntary, he has always regarded himself as bound by the same obligations as a paid officer of the State."

My youngest son Nawabzada Hamidullah Khan is still at college, and is working hard for his degree. By his studious habits, his polite manners, and his good behaviour, he has set an example to the youth of Bhopal which has contributed not a little to the success of my educational schemes. At the same time, by exemplifying the advantages of a mother's careful training, he has unconsciously provided an unanswerable argument in favour of female education.

During the period covered by this volume, there have been three ministers of the Revenue Department, namely, Khan Bahadur Mumtaz Ali Khan, Maulavi Nizam-ud-din Hasan, and Maulavi Nasir-ud-din. As I have already made frequent reference to the valuable work done by these three officers, I need not here do more than record my high appreciation of their services to the State. The present incumbent of the post is Maulavi Muhammad Ahmad, M.A., formerly Junior Secretary to the Board of Revenue in the United

Provinces. His abilities and past experience lead me to hope that he will discharge his duties no less successfully than his predecessors.

The post of Judicial Minister was held first by Maulavi Nasir-ud-din, and after him by its present occupant, Khan Bahadur Munshi Israr Hasan Khan. The former was an eminent lawyer, and, during his term of office, instituted many reforms in the department. Munshi Israr Hasan Khan is another officer whose services have received frequent mention, both in this and the preceding volumes of my memoirs. For a long time he held combined charge of the Judicial and the Police departments, both of which made marked progress under his management. Throughout his long and honourable connection with the State he has maintained the reputation of a loyal, energetic, reliable, and capable officer.

After the separation of the Judicial and Police departments, the latter was placed in, and is still under the charge of, Khan Bahadur Shaikh Muhammad Sarwar, whose services have been lent to the State by the Government of the Central Provinces. He is a very experienced officer, and is much thought of in the Central Provinces, where he worked his way from a humble to an important position by sheer merit. I am confident that the Police Department will make steady progress under his management.

Maulavi Syad-ud-din, who is now Assistant Revenue Minister, is a very old servant of the State.

He too, is a man of wide experience, having served some time or another in practically every department of the administration. His industry and ability have led to his gradual promotion to his present position. As a further mark of my favour, this year conferred upon him the title of "Bahadur". Of the other important posts in the Revenue Department, that of Director of Land Records is held by Munshi Mahmud Hasan Khan, B.A., and that of Conservator of Forests by Munshi Nazir Abbas. Both these officers are as yet new to their work, but I have every hope that they will justify their appointments.

Pandit Har Kishan is Customs Officer. He has held this post for two years, and great credit is due to him for the efficient manner in which he has carried out his important duties.

Amongst the officers of the Judicial Department, the following are deserving of mention for their meritorious work: Munshi Wahaj-ud-din, Barrister-at-Law, the Assistant Judicial Minister; Syad Liaqat Ali, M.A., LL.B., the Sadr-ul-muham; Syad Murtaza Ali, Barrister-at-Law, the Sadr-us-sudur; Syad Murtaza, the City Magistrate, and Mian Qadr Muhammad Khan, Honorary Magistrate.

Syad Liaqat Ali has held various State appointments, and has always been distinguished for his integrity and independence. He was for two years tutor to Nawabzada Hamidullah Khan in the earlier stage of his education. Mian Qadr Muhammad

Khan is my kinsman, being the great-grandson of the Nawab Jahangir Muhammad Khan, the ninth ruler of Bhopal. He is a young man of much intelligence and energy. I am very glad to see him taking an active part in the public life of Bhopal. He is the only descendant of Nawab Jahangir Muhammad Khan, outside my own family, who is serving the State in an honorary capacity.

I now come to my secretaries and the officers of my personal staff. The post of Chief Secretary is held by Munshi Avadh Bisaria, B.A. He was formerly Chief Accounts Officer, and in that capacity he made many salutary reforms in the Accounts Department, and especially in the State system of accountancy, which he did his best to bring into conformity with modern methods.

Munshi Abdur Rauf Khan holds the post of Political Secretary, or Durbar Vakil. I first took him into my employ when I was made heir-apparent, and he has served me in various capacities ever since. It was he who taught my eldest son English. Previous to his present appointment, he held for a time that of Judicial Secretary. Whatever the nature of his duties, he has always performed them with credit and I have complete confidence in him.

Munshi Syad Mansab Ali, who is Financial Secretary, has also been in my service since I became heir-apparent. He is intimately acquainted with the affairs of the State, and on many occasions his assistance has been of great value to me.

Munshi Wajid Ali, the Judicial Secretary, and Munshi Sakhawat Husain, my Private Secretary, have both discharged their duties with praiseworthy devotion. Munshi Sakhawat Husain was Assistant Private Secretary to my mother. He, therefore, came to me with plenty of experience, which stood me in good stead during the early, and in many respects the most trying, years of my reign.

Maulavi Ahmad Ibrahim is in charge of the miscellaneous branch of the Secretariat. Though he has but recently been appointed, I have formed a high opinion of his character and capabilities.

Mian Abdus Samad Khan, at present doing duty as Assistant Chief Secretary, is my step-nephew. He is a man of education and intelligence, and as I do not observe purdah with him, I find him of great assistance when I am going through the various files and State papers that have to be submitted to me. He and Abdul Hamid, who is a son of my foster-sister, are the only two officers who present papers to me personally.

Seth Hem Raj, the State cashier, and Seth Narayan Das, the Superintendent of the Treasury, are both officers of the highest integrity, and both are entitled to my thanks for valuable and faithful service.

Munshi Abdul Ghafur, B.A., is acting Superintendent of the Accounts Office. The work of this officer has always given me complete satisfaction. He was formerly, for a period of six years, Superintendent of the *tanzimat*, the office in which laws and regulations are drafted, or translated.

Mufti Anwar-ul-haqq, M.A., who was formerly one of my Under-Secretaries, is now Director of Public Instruction. He has done much to improve the schools of Bhopal, and has entered with energy and enthusiasm into all my plans for increasing the efficiency of the Educational Department, and extending the field of its operations. Mrs. Bakhsh and Mrs. Jowhari, the Lady Superintendents of the Sultania and the Victoria Girls' Schools, have worked hard and successfully for the institutions under their management. Mrs. Jowhari has not been long in Bhopal, but she has already proved herself a valuable acquisition to the Educational Department. Mrs. Bakhsh has been in charge of the Sultania School for the past five years. She is a thorough mistress of the art of teaching, and her tact, kindness, and sympathy, have enabled her to gain the confidence and affection of her pupils. I am very grateful to both these ladies for the work they have done for the cause of female education in Bhopal, a cause which I hold it to be my special mission to promote.

My honour's list would be incomplete without a reference to the Military Department, which has made great strides in last few years. Amongst the officers of this department, both Colonel Obaidullah Khan and I have been much pleased with the work of Sardar Bahadur Abdul Aziz Pasha, who has for some time been second in command of the State forces. Previous to entering the service of the State, he was a Risaldar in the Imperial army. He has proved himself a capable and thoroughly reliable officer, and has rendered much assistance in the reorganizing of the State army.

Major Mian Iqbal Muhammad Khan is my step-nephew. He joined the army at the request of Colonel Obaidullah Khan, who personally supervised his military education. I have always received very favourable reports of his diligence and the keen interest he takes in his duties. He is the only member of his branch of the Bhopal family to follow in the steps of his ancestors and adopt the profession of arms. Sardar Bahadur Major Mirza Karim Beg, M.V.O., was selected to command the Bhopal Victoria Lancers in the reign of my mother, and he still holds the same appointment. He is a highly trained and a most energetic officer. He represented the Bhopal State at the Diamond Jubilee of Her Majesty Queen Victoria, and when, in the year 1905, His Majesty King George, then Prince of Wales, visited India, he was placed in charge of His Majesty's baggage, for which service he was made a member of the Victorian Order.

Captain Amir Ahmad, M.V.O., after serving Colonel Obaidullah Khan in various capacities, has been given the appointment of Military

Secretary to the Commander-in-Chief. He has earned his rapid promotion from one post to another by his industry, versatility, and good behaviour, and by never neglecting an opportunity to make himself useful to his superiors. Those people who are ambitious to rise in the world will do well to take a leaf out of this officer's book.

Very excellent work has also been done by Major Abdul Qayum Khan, Major Imamullah Khan, Captain Hasan Ali, and other officers both of the Imperial Service Troops and of the State army, to whom I have not space to refer individually.

To all the above-mentioned servants of the State, and to the many others who have borne their share of the burden of administration, I tender my thanks for their loyal services. I hope that the high standard of duty which they have set up will be maintained, and that the State and the public will continue to reap the benefit of their zeal and efficiency.

CHAPTER XXIII

GENERAL SURVEY OF THE ADMINISTRATION

IT only remains for me to summarize, very briefly, the results of the various reforms I have made in the administration of the State since my accession. In the earlier years of my rule, the estimated income from land revenue was 28 *lakhs* of rupees; but the actual amount realized never exceeded 18 *lakhs*. At the present time the estimated income from the same source is slightly over 35½ *lakhs*. This increase is the direct outcome of the concessions made under the quinquennial settlement, which I introduced in 1903. Further, as a result of the regulations introduced under the nineteen years' settlement, the cultivators now pay their dues punctually and in full to the *mustajirs*, and the latter are equally punctual in their payments to the State. The ever-recurring problem, how to deal with arrears of payment, has been settled, I hope finally. As I have stated elsewhere, a part of the large sum due to the State was collected, and the remainder, amounting to considerably more than half the debt, was remitted. At the same time, new regulations to prevent the accumulation of arrears were brought into force. These have so far operated very successfully, and there is good ground for hoping that the State will not have to suffer from a difficulty of this nature again.

In many parts of the State there are signs that the cultivators are beginning to shake off their ancestral lethargy, and are making serious efforts to increase the value of their holdings. The Durbar is always ready to advance capital to deserving cultivators ; and a scheme for the opening of agricultural banks is at this time under consideration. Some idea of the progress that is taking place may be gained from last year's land statistics, which show that, during the year, 550,504 *bighas* of land were newly brought under cultivation.

The reorganization of the Forest Department, in which employment is now given only to those who have received training in forestry, has been productive of equally good results. The nett income derived from this department, which formerly amounted to Rs. 1,000, is at the present time close upon Rs. 70,000.

The income derived from the Customs Department has reached Rs. 6,87,025, the expenditure being Rs. 47,609. In the earlier part of my reign the expenditure was over Rs. 40,000, and the income was much nearer two *lakhs* of rupees than three. The income from the Excise Department has increased from about Rs. 40,000 to Rs. 1,58,500, while the expenditure is only

Rs. 13,357. This department is conducted on the "minimum guarantee" system.

I have described in the *Gohur-i-Ikbal* the financial position which I had to face when I ascended the throne. It will suffice, therefore, for me to mention that, in the last year of my mother's reign, the revenue of the State from all sources was only Rs. 18,00,000. This was very much less than the cost of the administration. On salaries alone the monthly expenditure exceeded two lakhs of rupees; and when I enquired into the state of the treasury, I found that my available resources amounted to the magnificent sum of Rs. 40,000. With the help of Almighty God, I managed to tide over this emergency, and by degrees I have been able to bring the finances of the State into a satisfactory condition. At any rate, I think I can guarantee that my successor will not have to start, as I did, with an empty exchequer.

I know that, according to the principles of political economy, money should not be allowed to lie idle, but should be profitably invested, or, at least, deposited in a bank, so that some income may be derived from it. There are, however, many Mussalmans who hold that to make profit out of investments is contrary to the teaching of Islam; and, though this view is often disputed, I consider it better that State money should not be employed in this way.

With a view to systematizing the work of

administration, I issued, during the first 12 years of my reign, 125 Acts. Of these, 66 dealt with the Revenue Department, 28 with the Judicial Department, and 18 were of a general character. 12 Acts were repealed during the same period. All Acts, orders and instructions, published by me from time to time, have been collected together, and issued in book form, for the information and guidance of the public.

The Judicial and Jail Departments were in a comparatively satisfactory state in my mother's reign. The final appeal in all cases was to the Wazir, the Ruler's confirmation being required only for sentences of death, or imprisonment for life. Since my accession I have taken care to see that only men with legal qualifications and experience are appointed to this department. I have also taken steps for the general speeding up of the legal machinery, with the result that at the close of the year 1912 there were, in all the courts of the State, only 84 cases undisposed of, as compared with 1,110 such cases in the first year of my reign. I myself gave judgment in 347 cases.

In the Police Department, regulations regarding the height and age of recruits have been issued, a new uniform has been adopted, and the whole police force has been rearmed with modern carbines purchased from the arsenals of the Government of India. Every recruit has now to pass a medical test, and undergoes a regular course of training in drill and musketry. Salaries have been considerably increased. Formerly the pay of a constable was Rs. 5 per mensem, and that of a sub-inspector, Rs. 20, rising to Rs. 30. Under present regulations a constable's pay rises to Rs. 8. A head constable receives Rs. 10 to Rs. 30, and a sub-inspector Rs. 30 to Rs. 50. The question of still further increasing these salaries is under consideration.

The supervision exercised by police outposts, chowkidars, and patrols affords ample security for both life and property. In addition to the regular police force, which now numbers 2,647 men, a corps of boys has been formed in which the sons of policemen are enrolled. These lads are trained to do duty as orderlies, and many of them eventually enter the police force.

In 1909, on the occasion of Lord Minto's visit to Bhopal, the officers of the Government of India, who came in advance to inspect the police arrangements, remarked as follows :

> "The Bhopal police are superior to those of any other State. Indeed some of their officers and sepoys are as smart and capable as any that could be found amongst the Government police throughout India."

Mr. Waterfield, the Inspector-General of Police in Central India, congratulated Munshi Israr Hasan Khan, under whose charge the department then was, on the admirable arrangements he had made. And Mr. Douglas Straight, Inspector-

General of Police in the United Provinces, in the course of a letter to the Munshi Sahib, wrote :

" As regards the Police arrangements we can congratulate ourselves on the co-operation of the Government and the State Police, and we may be thankful that everything passed off satisfactorily, after the Ahmedabad experience. In appearance I consider your police are quite the best I have so far seen in any Native State, and I was much struck with the excellent way the traffic regulations were carried out, and the intelligence shown both by officers and men. You are in every way to be congratulated on having such a fine force of men, which is no doubt due in great measure to your personal administration."

The same gentleman remarked in a letter to the Political Agent :

" I was very much struck with what I saw, and have obtained quite a new idea of the Police in advanced Native States."

When Lord Hardinge visited Bhopal this year, full confidence was placed in the State Police, and His Excellency gave a present to the officer in charge to signify his appreciation of the arrangements made.

Much has been done in the way of prison reform, and prisoners live under much better and more sanitary conditions than was formerly the case. They are given instruction in various arts and industries such as the manufacture of carpets and durries, carpentry, knitting by machinery, and horticulture. This enables them, when they are released, to find employment, and lead honest lives ; and that many are thus benefited is shown by the fact that second convictions have become much rarer than they used to be.

The progress of education in the State may be gauged from the fact that in the city of Bhopal to-day there are more than 600 students in the English teaching schools, and over 850 in the Madrasa-i-Sulaimania, where only vernacular instruction is given. About 100 boys attend the Technical School. This institution is as yet in an early stage of development; but it is making good progress, and is already attracting students from outside the State.

There is a special Madrasa for religious instruc tion where the curriculum of studies is the same as that followed in the famous religious seminary at Deoband. Examinations are held yearly under the supervision of the Ulama of Deoband, who grant *sanads* to the successful candidates. Affiliated to this Madrasa is another for the instruction of those who aspire to the title, *hafiz*.[1] At the beginning of my reign the number of students attending these Madrasas was 650. The number has since risen to 1,600. In the English Schools special arrangements are made for religious instruction, which is given a definite place in the curricula of studies. Very good work continues to be done by the Madrasa-i-tibbiya, or Medical School. The teaching is of a thoroughly practical kind, and deals with both medicine and surgery.

1 Hafiz (*lit.* a guardian or protector) is the title given to one who has committed the whole Quran to memory.

The two principal institutions for the education of girls are the Victoria and the Sultania Schools. The former, which has been in existence for many years, is a primary school, and the latter, which has been established during my own reign, gives instruction up to the middle-school standard. A school, modelled on the Sultania, has recently been opened at Sehore, and another, called The Birjisia Kanya Pathshala, for the instruction of Hindu girls only, has been opened at Bhopal. In all, about 400 girls are receiving instruction, and the need for additional schools is daily becoming more apparent.

The State now devotes over a *lakh* of rupees annually to education, and a further sum of ten thousand rupees is spent every year on scholarships. These are given to assist students to qualify themselves in medicine, engineering, agriculture, law, and other sciences, or to enable them to proceed to Europe for more advanced study. Several scholarship-holders are at the present time reading in the Aligarh College, one is in England learning accountancy, and two others are on their way to Europe. Many orphan girls are receiving instruction in nursing and midwifery at the Lady Lansdowne Hospital. There is now an Infant Home attached to the Hospital in which orphan and destitute children are housed, fed, and clothed. When old enough to leave the home, the boys are sent to the Sulaimania School, and the girls are trained as midwives or nurses.

Since my accession many additions have been made to the public buildings of Bhopal. These include the Revenue Courts, the Courts of Justice, the Minto Hall, the Civil Club and the Hamidia Library, all handsome structures, which have added much to the beauty and dignity of the city. Numerous residential bungalows have also been built on the margins of the lakes and in other picturesque situations. These, with their tastefully laid out compounds, constitute another attractive feature of modern Bhopal. The main thoroughfares have been widened and greatly improved in appearance by the demolition of unsightly and dilapidated houses. In many cases the sites thus acquired have been preserved as open spaces, or made into gardens for the benefit of the public.

In the *mofussil* new roads have been made, and others are under construction. I hope that, in the near future, metalled high-ways will traverse every district of the State. Special attention has been given to village sanitation. The sanitary arrangements in every *tahsil* are supervised by officers of the Bhopal Municipality. Both in the *mofussil* and in the city of Bhopal women have been appointed to act as sanitary inspectors of purdah dwellings.

As a rule, the upkeep of a town is paid for out of the rates levied on the inhabitants. In the town of Bhopal, however, where the large majority of the inhabitants are in poor circumstances, the rates imposed are very few, and the income derived from them seldom exceeds Rs. 18,000. The average annual expenditure of the Municipality is about Rs. 66,000; so that every year there is a deficit of nearly Rs. 50,000, which is made good from the coffers of the State.

As a result of the extensive reforms that have been taken in hand by the Military Department, the forces of the State have been brought to a high state of efficiency. To maintain troops in such a condition is necessarily a costly business; yet although both the State army and the Imperial Service Troops are better trained and better equipped than they have ever been before, the expenditure on account of the Military Department is actually less to-day than it was in the first year's of my rule. This very satisfactory state of affairs is to be attributed to the ability with which General Obaidullah Khan has carried out his duties as Commander-in-Chief.

Amongst the miscellaneous administrative measures which I have introduced I may mention the preparation of a yearly budget, the grading of State officers, and the issue of a revised scale of salaries and promotions. The monthly expenditure on salaries is nearly double what it was in former days. The offices of the various departments have been remodelled on modern lines; new systems of filing papers and of keeping accounts have been introduced; and in every office of any importance, the old-fashioned cushions and pillows have been replaced by chairs and tables.

By means such as these I have been constantly seeking to bring order and increased efficiency into the administration of my State. I render thanks to Almighty God for His mercies, and I pray for His guidance and protection in the years to come.

INDEX

Abdul Aziz Pasha, 181, 198.
Abdul Ghafur, Maulavi, 234, 243.
Abdul Jabbar Khan, Maulavi, 21.
Abdur Rauf Khan, Munshi, 242.
Abdu-s Samad Mazhar, 10, 185, 243.
Abru Begam, 45.
Aden, 85.
Aftab Ahmad Khan, Sahibzada, 160.
Aftab Begam, 28, 46.
Aga Khan, the, 115.
Akbar, Emperor, 19.
Alexandra, Queen, 80-81, 140-143.
Alexandra School, 3, 6, 29, 47-49, 93, 119, 200, 201.
Aligarh, 90, 92-96.
Allahabad Exhibition, 114-115, 124, 125, 230.
Amir Ahmad, Captain, 36, 63, 182, 245.
Antrim, Lady, 37, 143.
Anwar-ul-haqq, Mufti, 200, 244.
Aquil Muhammad Khan, Mian, 35, 39, 225, 226.
Arcot, Prince of, 17.
Ashta, 135.
Atia Fyzi, Miss, 45, 46, 115.
Avadh Bisaria Munshi, 242.

Bakhsh, Mrs., 43, 121, 137, 244.
Bakhshi Muhammad Hasan, 228.
Barnes, Mrs., 23, 24-26, 84, 88, 91. 137.
Benares, 84.
Benazir Palace, 29.
Bhavnagar, Maharani of, 178.
Bhopal, City of, 33, 130–131, 255-256.
Birjis Jahan Begam, Sahibzadi. 41, 43, 64-66, 89, 102, 107-108. QWI 128-129, 137.
Birjisia Kanya Pathshala, School, 254.
Blong, Miss, 24.
Bombay, 13, 85, 91, 112, 154, 184.
Brindisi, 152.
Brown, Mrs., 88-89.
Budapest. 148, 151.
Buckingham Palace, 139, 145, 146

Cairo, 153, 154.
Calcutta, 78, 83-84, 186-188.
Canning, Lord, 127.
Census, 22.
Connaught, Duke of, 145, 146.
Coronation of King George V, 144-145, 184.
Coronation celebrations at Bhopal, 184.
Cotton Mills, 221-222.
Council of State, 16.
Creagh, Lady, 106, 187, 192.
———, Sir O'Moore, 106, 192-193.
Customs Department, 248.

Daly College, Indore, 7, 92, 111, 193-194.

Daly, Colonel Hugh, 7, 31, 53, 61, 62, 64-70, 90, 97-101, 193-194.

——, Sir Henry, 98, 99.

——, Mrs., 58, 62, 68, 69, 100.

Dancing parties, 3.

Dane, Sir Louis, 105.

Darshan Jharokha, 174.

Delhi, 159-181, 218.

Devonshire, Duchess of, 178, 183.

Diwangang, 21, 131-132.

Dolma Baghchah Palace, 149.

Dover, 138.

Drummond, General, 60-64, 182.

Dufferin, Lady, 215.

Durbar, the Imperial, 157, 168-170,

Earl, Mrs., 106.

Education, Female, 27, 44-45, 120, 121, 200, 202, 211, 223, 236, 254.

———— of Indian Chiefs, 6-8, 92, 100, 111-112, 211.

————, Primary, 74-75.

Educational Conference, All India, 159-161.

Educational Department, 134-135, 223, 253-254.

Edward VII, King, 29, 76-82, 88-89.

Edward Museum, 29-30, 49-50, 119.

Elliot, Lady Eileen, 37, 43, 107, 143.

Excise Department, 12, 248.

Fasli Calendar, 18, 72.

Faujdar Muhammad Khan, Mian, 206.

Florence, 152.

Forest Department, 12, 20, 248.

Geneva, 148.

George V, King, 76, 81-82, 123, 139, 140, 144-146, 161-165, 168-185.

Grimston, General, 62, 176.

Gwalior State, 72 232.

————, Maharaja of, 100, 231-232,

————, Maharani 10, 190.

Habibullah Khan, Sahibzada, 41, 64-66, 103, 104.

Haig, Major, 84.

Hamidia Library, 196, 200-203.

Hamidullah Khan, Sahibzada 11, 16, 36, 37, 38, 48, 65, 90, 92-95, 108, 135, 137, 139, 141, 174, 199, 201, 203, 207, 217-218, 237, 239.

Hardinge, Lord, Viceroy, 123, 156, 157, 165-166, 169, 171, 177-178, 186-187, 193-214, 216, 219.

————, first Lord, 195, 201, 202, 205, 206, 208, 213.

————, Lady, 169, 170, 177, 178, 186-187, 189, 197, 199, 203, 204, 214-217.

Hardinge Military School, 212-214.

Har Kishen, Pandit, 241.

Harman Singh, 105, 106.

Hazrat Usman, 150, 151.

Hewett, Sir John, 114, 115, 230.

Hit Karini Sabha, 133.

Hoare, Mr., 67, 69.

Hyde, Mr., 193, 194.

Hyderabad, Nizam, of, 190.

Ichawar, 134.

Id-ul-fitr, 152.

Ihtisham-ul-mulk, Nawab, 10, 28.

Imperial Service Troops, 15-16, 55, 59-64, 125, 158, 182, 210, 224.

Infants' Home, Bhopal, 196, 214-216.

Iqbal Muhammad Khan, Mian, 10 245.

Islamia Orphanage Calcutta, 187-188.

Israr Hasan Khan, Nasir-ud-din, 17, 34, 38, 59-64, 125, 158, 182, 210, 224.

Jagirdars, 2, 14, 72, 133-134, 226.
Jahangiria School, 37, 119.
Jahangir Muhammad Khan, Nawab, 206, 226.
Jammu, Maharaja of, 190.
Janjira, Begam Sahiba of, 115, 117.
Jenkins, Lady, 187.
Jowhari, Mrs., 244.
Judicial Department, 72-73, 124, 250.

Kapurthala, Maharaja of, 230.
Karim Beg, Major Mirja, 35, 39, 63, 245.
Khedive, H. H. the, 153.
Kindergarten classes, 135.
Kitchener, Lord, 8, 15, 146, 153, 154.
Korwai, Nawab of, 194.

Ladies Club, Bhopal, 27-29, 45-47, 122, 143, 204, 235.
Land Records Office, 70.
Lansdowne Hospital, 23, 43, 211.
Liak'at Ali, Syad, 11, 241.
Lucknow, 84.
Lukis, Surg.-General, 106-107.

Mansab Ali, Syad, 10, 36, 154, 242.
M. A. O. College, Aligarh, 55, 90. 96, 218, 234.
Marseilles, 137.
Mary, Queen, 28, 139; 140, 144, 145, 161, 168-174, 176, 178, 180, 181, 183, 188-189.
McMahon, Sir Henry, 162, 165, 232-233.
Medical School, Bhopal, 253.
Military Department, 15, 54, 55, 125, 224, 239, 244-246, 256.
Military School, Bhopal, 196.
Minto Hall, Bhopal, 57.
Minto, first Lord, 32, 51, 54.
——, Lord, Viceroy, 31-58, 83, 104-107, 112, 113, 122-123, 143.
Minto, Lady, 22-23, 36, 37, 39, 43-47, 58, 83, 103-105, 107, 143, 146, 215.
Muhammad Hasan Khan, 19.
Muhammad Sarwar Khan, 191, 240.
Mumtaz Husain Khan, Risaldar, 63.
Mushtaq Husain, Nawab, 94.
Mussoorie, 77, 86-90.
Mustajirs, 14, 18-21, 73, 124, 131-132, 247.

Naidu, Mrs., 160.
Narsingarh, Raja Sahib of, 47, 197, 199.
Nasir-ud-din, Maulavi, 30, 49, 67, 154, 158, 227, 239, 240.
Nasrullah Khan, Nawab, 3, 30, 36, 38, 49, 53, 55, 63-65, 70, 126, 137, 153, 154, 158, 174, 180, 207, 212, 220, 224, 238.
Nauheim, 138.
Nur Jahan Begam, Sahibzadi, 70
Nursing School, Bhopal, 23, 196, 214.
Nur-ul-hasan, Hakim, 91, 152, 228-229.

Obaidullah Khan, Colonel, 8, 11, 15, 34, 36, 38, 40, 56-57, 59-64, 66, 69, 83-91, 95, 106, 108, 126, 137, 139, 145, 175-176, 180, 207, 212, 224-225, 237.
O'Dwyer, Mr. M. F., 109-111, 119, 122, 125-128.
Opium, cultivation of, 12.
Orcha, Maharani of, 174.
Ormuz, 58, 135.

Pachmarhi, 75.
Paris, 137-138.
Partabgarh, Rani of, 116.
Pattison Court, 139.
Payne, Mr., 36, 47, 94.
Piklon, *tahsil*, 131-132.

Pitcher, Captain, 62.
Plague at Bhopal, 13, 153, 159, 223.
Police Department, 124, 191, 250. 252.
Porter, Mrs., 115, 116, 233.
Port Said, 137, 152, 153, 154.
Postal Department, 4-6.

Qadr Muhammad Khan, Mian, 241-242.
Qaisar Dulhan Sahiba, 41, 189, 204.
Qudsia Begam, Nawab, 131, 179.

Rafiqullah Khan, Sahibzada, 41, 65, 169.
Raghio Bey, 148.
Rajgarh, Raja Sahib of, 47, 197, 199.
Rajpur, 87, 90.
Redhil, 139, 143, 158.
Religious Instruction, School of, 253.
Revenue Administration, 9-10, 13-14, 18-21, 124, 131-133, 206-207, 222, 247.
Roberts, Colonel, 84, 85, 86, 113.
Rudra, Miss, 122.
Ryatwari System, 132.

Sakhawat Husain, Munshi, 11, 35, 86, 243.
Sanchi, 109, 159, 203.
Shah Bano Begam, 41, 136, 189, 204.
Shah Jahan Begam, Nawab, 51, 179.
Shahriar Dulhan Sahiba, 41, 86, 87, 95, 137, 189, 204.
Shams-ul-ulama, Maulana, 236-237.
Sikandar Begam, Nawab, 51, 53, 127, 195-196, 206, 209, 228.
Simla, 101-108.
Sinha, Mr., 79.
Siyahat-i-sultani, 136.
Smith, Colonel Dunlop, 138, 139, 140, 142.
Sorabji, Miss, 117.
Sultania Infantry, 224.
Sultania School, 43-45, 119-121, 125, 203, 211, 223.
Sultan Jahan Begam, H. H. Nawab, *vide* Table of Contents, pp. vii-xiii.
Syad-ud-din, Maulavi, 240-241.
Syad Nur-ul-hasan, Hakim, 91, 228-229.
Sydenham, Lord, 232.

Taqavi System, 71-72, 134.
Technical School, 253.
Teck, Duke of, 170.
Thakur Laran Singh, 133.
Therapia, 148, 150.
Towle, Mr. J. H. 94.
Tucker, Mr. A. L. P., 193, 232.
Turkey, Sultan of, 148, 149, 151.
———, Sultana of, 148, 149, 150.
Tuzuk-i-sultani, 112.

Victoria Lancers, 175, 224.
Victoria, Princess, 142, 145.
———, Queen, 165, 179-180.
Victoria School, 46, 119, 121-122, 203, 211, 244.
Viqar-ul-mulk, Nawab, 94, 96, 160.

Wahid-uz-zafar Khan, Sahibzada, 41, 65, 137, 169.
Wales, the Prince of, 144, 145.
Wali Muhammad, Mr., 137.
Wazir Muhammad Khan, Nawab, 51, 103, 104.
Wood, Mr. G. B., 104, 108.

Yar Muhammad Khan, Mian, 35, 225.
Yasin Muhammad Khan, Mian, 35, 225.

Zulfiqar Ali Khan, Nawab, 105, 106.